Peonies

Pamela McGeorge
Photographs by Russell McGeorge

FIREFLY BOOKS

PAGE 1: *Paeonia mlokosewitschii.* PAGE 2: Peonies, Gore Public Gardens, Southland, New Zealand. *PAGE 3: 'Bravura'. ABOVE:* An unnamed peony cultivar. *OPPOSITE (FROM TOP): Paeonia mascula* ssp. *mascula;* unnamed tree peony hybrid; 'Coral Charm'; *Paeonia rockii;* 'Perfection'.

Acknowledgements

Writing a book about flowers, and taking photographs to illustrate it, is always an enjoyable project. When the flowers are as extravagantly beautiful as peonies, an extra dimension is added to the experience. None of it would have happened without the generous help of those growers throughout the South Island of New Zealand who shared their gardens and their knowledge with us.

As always, our thanks go to Pat and Keith Stuart of Wanaka. Their garden is a continuing inspiration in our work. To Dot and John McFarlane and their family, of Waimate, thank you for your peonies—both the tree peonies and the glorious fields of 'Coral Sunset'—your friendly hospitality, and your insights into commercial production of peonies on a large scale; to Tony and Judy Banks of Omeo Peonies in Alexandra, for sharing your gorgeous garden and stunning peonies; to Julie Allan of Marsal Peonies, in Canterbury, for all the photographs at your peony farm; to Jane Sutherland of Timaru for the wonder of your tree peony blooms; to Paul and Esther Simmons of Christchurch for your extensive array of peonies and your time; to Jan and Trudi Heemskerk who 'adopted' us in the Netherlands and took us to a fabulous peony show in Keukenhof, and to all the numerous gardening friends in Wanaka who rang us when their peonies were picture-perfect, our sincere appreciation. Finally, a big thank you to Tracey Borgfeldt and Andrea Hassall at David Bateman, who kept us on track during the long production process but missed out on the fun parts.

A FIREFLY BOOK

Published by Firefly Books Ltd. 2006

First printing

Publisher Cataloging-in-Publication Data (U.S.)

McGeorge, Pamela, 1943-
    Peonies / Pamela McGeorge ;
photographs by Russell McGeorge.
—1st ed.
[144] p. : col. photos. ; cm.
Includes bibliographical references and index.
Summary: Introductory guide to growing hundreds of species, varieties and hybrids of peonies. Provides practical advice on how to plant, propagate, cultivate and landscape peonies.
ISBN-13: 978-1-55407-168-5 (pbk.)
ISBN-10: 1-55407-168-2 (pbk.)
1. Peonies. 2. Peonies —Varieties. I. McGeorge, Russell, 1943-
II. Title.
635.9/3362 21   SB413.P4M34   2006

Library and Archives Canada Cataloguing in Publication

McGeorge, Pamela, 1943-
Peonies / Pamela McGeorge ; photographs by Russell McGeorge.
Includes bibliographical references and index.
ISBN-13: 978-1-55407-168-5
ISBN-10: 1-55407-168-2
1. Peonies. I. McGeorge, Russell, 1943- II. Title.
SB413.P4M33 2006   635.9'3362   C2006-900475-7

Published in the United States by
Firefly Books (U.S.) Inc.
P.O. Box 1338, Ellicott Station
Buffalo, New York 14205

Published in Canada by
Firefly Books Ltd.
66 Leek Crescent
Richmond Hill, Ontario L4B 1H1

First published in 2006 by
David Bateman Ltd.,
30 Tarndale Grove,
Albany, Auckland, New Zealand

Design Jag Graphics
Printed in China through Colorcraft Ltd., Hong Kong

CONTENTS

Introduction

PREVIOUS PAGES: 'Coral Sunset' in full bloom.

ABOVE: Ready to go. An innovative way to display peonies. Photographed at the Peony Growers' Show at Keukenhof, Lisse, the Netherlands.

Extravagant language seems to be the hallmark of peony lovers. Since we first started to look at plants for their beauty, and not just for their healing properties, peonies have basked in our admiration. Words echo down the centuries, recording the impressions that peonies have made on those who have grown and loved them.

"We cherish them for the beauty and delight of their goodly flowers," wrote Englishman John Parkinson, herbalist to the king and apothecary of the time, in 1629.

"The most superb and commanding flower which the garden holds," wrote Alice Harding, doyenne of American peony growers, in 1917.

"The fattest and most scrumptious of all flowers, a rare fusion of fluff and majesty," wrote garden writer extraordinaire, Henry Mitchell, in the later years of the 20th century.

No peony grower today would argue with these descriptions, and such is the magic of these flowers that they have seduced gardeners for more than 20 centuries—long before the massive and spectacular modern hybrids we grow today had appeared on the scene.

Peonies are divided into two main groups: herbaceous varieties, which die down in the fall; and tree peonies, which are deciduous but whose woody structure remains during winter—like the skeleton of any deciduous tree. Both bear extravagantly sumptuous flowers.

In China, the peony has been consistently treasured down through the ages. In the West its fortunes have fluctuated. First praised for its beauty in 1629, it gradually fell victim to its success. The wealthy classes came to consider a plant that lasted the lifetime of a human being, and available to all, as vulgar and common. They wanted rare plants, things that were difficult to grow, and the peony for a time was known as a "poor man's flower." However, during the 19th century, as the number of named cultivars with spectacular flowers increased, the popularity of peonies rose. They became symbolic of the stylish Edwardian times before their decline set in once again.

As the 20th century unrolled, the impetus for developing new peonies moved from Europe to the United States. American breeders began producing a series of handsome cultivars, both herbaceous and tree varieties, and more growers entered the market. In the last years of the 20th century, as China increasingly opened its doors to the West, new species were discovered, and Chinese varieties have been exported, adding to the pool of available plants. That trend continues.

Today, herbaceous peonies increasingly are taking a large share of the cut-flower market, and named plants are sought after across international borders. Westerners go to China in the peony season to view vast plantings of this flower that has featured for so long in Chinese art and history. In the 21st century the peony in the Western world has come close to attaining the status and desirability it has always held in Chinese society.

This book is for gardeners who have already been seduced by peonies and want to find out how to choose the best varieties and care for them in their own gardens. It looks at the origins of peonies and highlights the efforts of early hybridizers. Some of the plants they produced are still popular today, more than 150 years after their first appearance on the market.

The book also discusses intersectional hybrids, a cross between tree peonies and herbaceous varieties, and introduces readers to the species, of which few gardeners are aware. Long neglected in favor of their flamboyant descendants, the species produce simpler, sometimes more elegant flowers that appeal to modern gardeners. Both plants and seeds are more available now than ever before, especially in the United States.

A list of suppliers is provided on pages 139–142. Many publish their selections or catalogs on the Internet. As with most popular flowers, new peony cultivars are constantly appearing, and suppliers can provide the most up-to-date information on which cultivars or species are available in any given season.

TOP: **Peonies on show at Keukenhof, in the Netherlands.**
ABOVE: **Bud burst.**

1 What Exactly Are Peonies?

Peonies come in a vast array of colors and forms. Think peony, and most people probably imagine the double cerise-red flowers our grandmothers used to grow. But there are also voluptuous, perfumed confections with raised centers like a mound of frilled lace, and yet others that come with a clarity of form that is heart-stopping in its simplicity.

Colors range from deepest, darkest crimson through every known shade of pink to salmon, yellow, cream and coral. Peonies also come in pristine white with crinkled petals as fragile as tissue paper. Depending on the individual plant and weather conditions, peonies will flower as early as April or as late as July (or from September to December in the Southern Hemisphere).

Tree peonies, which start blooming a week or two earlier than herbaceous peonies, have huge flowers shot with complex color combinations that are almost impossible to photograph consistently. It's no wonder that they have been revered in the East for centuries.

Nomenclature

The plant world is full of fascination for a wide group of people. Gardeners are usually most interested in the flowers and the foliage that plants produce; horticulturists are often more concerned with productivity and hybridization.

OPPOSITE: 'Illini Warrior', a shorter-than-average herbaceous peony.

RIGHT: 'Picotee' is an early-flowering Saunders' hybrid.

Dendrologists focus on trees and herbalists on the medicinal qualities of plants. But it is the botanists who study all aspects of plants—seeds, roots, flowers, foliage and growing habits—and assign them to families. And it's the botanists we blame when we suddenly find that the name of a well-loved plant has changed or that it has suddenly joined another family—usually because of an academic disagreement or because new knowledge has come to light. Nowadays, DNA testing allows for even more precise analyses and is yet another reason why many plants are being reclassified.

As with people, plant species need names to identify them and link them to other members in the same family. The classification system we use today was developed in the 18th century by Swedish botanist Carl Linnaeus (who Latinized his own name). He gave each plant two names in Latin form. The first, that of the genus, is equivalent to our family name. The second is descriptive and serves the same purpose as a person's given name—it denotes a specific individual. Together these two Latin tags identify a particular species. The system is international and works so well that it has not been replaced.

A broad grouping to which a plant belongs is the family. As with humans, there may be other closely related groups—cousins if you like—all members of the same large clan, but with distinguishing features that put them in different subgroups or genera.

The genus *Paeonia*

Peonies have a less complicated clan structure than many other plants. They used to be classified as members of the Ranunculaceae family, with the genus being *Paeonia*. Now they have a family all to themselves—the Paeoniaceae.

Within the genus *Paeonia* there are further divisions into species or subgroups of peonies with common characteristics. For example, *Paeonia officinalis* is a species of peony in the genus *Paeonia*, in the family Paeoniaceae.

Many of the species are divided yet again, into varieties or cultivars. 'Crimson Globe' is a variety of *Paeonia officinalis*, which means that it is derived from the species but, through various pollinations, its form and color have changed in different ways. Over the centuries, varieties of peony that occurred in nature have been selected by people, named and propagated. Others have been hand-pollinated, with the propagator aiming to achieve specific characteristics.

When two different species of peony are crossed, the result is a new creation called a hybrid, also usually created in an attempt to capture the best characteristics of both parents. 'Early Windflower' is a cross between *Paeonia emodi* and *P. veitchii* and exhibits characteristics of both species.

If the actual clan structure of peonies is less complicated than some other plants, there is ongoing confusion about the classification of species within the peony family. Botanists are often categorized as "lumpers" or "splitters"—those

OPPOSITE: Paeonia mlokosewitschii is a variable species. Most often a pale yellow, it also comes in white and pinky-buff shades.

BELOW: Called simply 'Dad', this peony is for those who like strong colors and uncomplicated shapes.

who tend to lump several similar plants into one species, or those who prefer to look at every minuscule difference and recognize it by assigning a specific name to each similar plant.

At the time of writing, it is generally accepted that there are a few more than 30 peony species, with some botanists treating a particular plant as a subspecies that another botanist might consider a species in its own right.

Peonies are divided into two distinct groups—the herbaceous variety and tree peonies. In 1992, in a radical new thesis written by Chinese botanist Hong Tao and several colleagues, the previously accepted wisdom concerning the identification of the progenitors of tree peonies was turned upside down, with the result that a long-recognized species name, *Paeonia suffruticosa*, which encompassed varieties that differed widely, has given way to several separate species names clarifying distinctions between varying plants.

The genus as a whole occurs in five disparate areas: the Mediterranean region; central Asia from the Urals to Siberia; the western Himalaya; eastern Asia from southwestern China to Manchuria and Japan; and Pacific North America.

European peonies are derived predominantly from *Paeonia officinalis*, a herbaceous species whose natural habitat stretches from northern Italy into Switzerland and France, and through former Yugoslavia, Hungary and Austria. Wild plants of this species are now very rare. The species and its varieties bloom early in the season, have only one bud per stem and are not noted for their perfume.

Chinese herbaceous peonies are varieties of the species *Paeonia lactiflora*. In the 19th century, when they were introduced to the West, they won the affections of gardeners because of their fragrance and the fact that each stem bears more than one bud, giving it a longer season of bloom. (The species *Paeonia emodi* and *P. veitchii* also produce side buds, resulting in several flowers per stem.) *Lactiflora* varieties have a wider range of color and form than their *officinalis* relations, and they flower later in the season. These two species have given birth to literally thousands of cultivars. In contrast, the two North American species, *Paeonia californica* and *P. brownii*, have had little impact on the development of garden plants.

Then there are the tree peonies, often known as "moutan" and somewhat neglected by Western gardeners until recently. Now they are gaining recognition, especially in the United States, for their breathtakingly beautiful flowers. The Chinese, however, have revered them for more than a millennium and long ago named them the "King of Flowers." Over the centuries both the Chinese and the Japanese have produced innumerable varieties, all of them derived from species whose homes are in various parts of China. See Chapter 8 for more on tree peonies.

OPPOSITE: Looking like crumpled satin, 'Eliza Lundy' is slow to fully open.

BELOW: The voluptuous beauty of this tree peony bloom helps to explain why the Chinese have revered these plants for centuries.

BOTTOM: Once open, 'Eliza Lundy' shows her *officinalis* parentage.

'Coral Sunset' in all its guises.

Color and fragrance

The color of peony flowers is frequently affected by age and exposure to sun. The fiercer the sun, the faster the color will fade. The enormously popular 'Coral Sunset' opens a rich coral and fades to an antique cream over several days. Immature plants often produce flowers of unexpected colors.

Many peonies are renowned for their fragrance, and some were actually used in perfumes at the beginning of the 20th century. As always, recognition of perfume is a personal reaction and some peonies can actually exude an unpleasant smell. In this book, where a peony is noted as fragrant, this is a generally reported perception as I am notoriously unable to detect a wide variety of fragrances.

Anatomy of a peony

Structure of the plant

The herbaceous peony is a perennial plant consisting of a crown planted underground, and from this all the growth originates. The storage roots are fleshy and bulbous, growing down and out and becoming more intertwined as the plant ages. Fine feeder roots spread out from the storage roots. In some species, the roots taper gradually to a point; in others, there are several storage roots, like small potatoes, joined to the central crown by a small stem. The species *Paeonia tenuifolia* spreads by stolons or above-ground runners.

The eyes from which new stems grow in the following year are formed at the base of the existing stems, after flowering has finished. In fall, the leaves wither and the plant dies down completely, remaining dormant over winter. Come spring, energy returns to the herbaceous peony. Previously formed buds on the underground crown begin to elongate, emerging as furled, bronzy-red shoots which develop into the structure of the plant for that season. Each year, as the plant matures, it puts forth more stems—sometimes as many as 30 on a well-established bush.

Young stems may be green, red or pink, though most turn green as the season progresses. If a bud or young stem is damaged early in the season, it will be replaced from a dormant eye that is stirred into action by the emergency.

The foliage of different species varies in color and form—from the almost grassy, finely cut bright green leaves of *Paeonia tenuifolia* to the broadly dissected leaves of *P. macrophylla* or *P. wittmanniana*. Some leaves are a bright, fresh green; some have a bluish cast; and others display red or bronze shadings.

The flowers open from tight, ball-shaped buds that develop at the end of long stems and vary in size from 2 in. (5 cm) to 10 in. (25 cm). The main flowering time varies from early spring to early summer—May to June in the Northern Hemisphere, late September to November in the Southern Hemisphere—with a few species flowering earlier.

Some species grow no taller than 12 in. (30 cm), but when fully grown most varieties develop into a bush that is from 3 to 4 ft. (1 to 1.2 m) tall and wide.

Tree peonies, in spite of their name, are in fact spreading, woody shrubs with long fibrous roots. When fully grown, they vary in height between 4 ft. and 8 ft. (1.2–2.4 m) and are a similar width. Their large and unimaginably beautiful flowers start to appear a couple of weeks earlier than those of the herbaceous varieties and include a wondrous selection of colors. Once the flowers have faded, their deeply dissected foliage remains as a feature until fall, when they lose their leaves, but their woody structure remains above ground through winter.

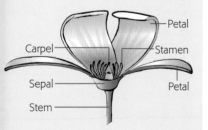

SECTIONAL VIEW OF A PEONY FLOWER

Petal — Carpel — Stamen — Sepal — Petal — Stem

Flowers and seeds

As explained by Harold E. Wolfe in *The Peonies*, a publication of the American Peony Society, wild peonies all produce complete flowers, meaning that they have four sets of parts: *sepals*, *petals*, *stamens* (the male organs) and *pistils* (the female organs; more usually referred to as *carpels* when peonies are the plant under discussion). Single cultivated blooms are also complete.

A flower is said to be incomplete when any of the four parts is missing. Double peonies are usually incomplete (although they may be exquisitely beautiful) as most have no carpels and no stamens—these have been transformed into *staminodes* or *petalodes*, which are not pollen bearing and look like finely shredded petals. From the hybridizer's point of view, the sexual parts are necessary for creating new varieties, although a flower that lacks stamens but contains carpels, such as the Japanese forms, can be used as a seed parent.

Anthers are tiny, oval, pollen-bearing structures, supported on slender stalks called *filaments*. Together they make up the stamens. When the anthers are ripe they open and release (or dehisce) huge numbers of pollen grains. Charles Darwin estimated that a single peony bloom might release three million!

The carpels or seedpods often form an attractive feature in the center of the flower, occasionally repeating the color of the petals. They are vase-shaped, divided usually into five separate vessels, each of which holds an ovary. As the flower ages, the stigma at the tip of the carpel becomes sticky, indicating that it is ready to receive pollen.

As they ripen, the seedpods turn from green to a brownish color and can be quite decorative. Some are slightly curved and have a furry coat. A peony seed is about the size of a pea and is surrounded by a hard, dark, shiny coat. The seedpods of *Paeonia mlokosewitschii* are particularly decorative, with brilliant infertile red and fertile black seeds exposed when the pod splits.

Peony seeds have specific dormancy requirements. Sow seed in a warm, moist location and it will readily send out a root, but the shoot will not appear above ground until the seed has undergone a dormancy period caused by dropping temperatures. When the soil temperatures warm up again the shoot will appear.

Flower forms

For the sake of identification of cultivars and the definition of categories on the show bench, herbaceous peony flowers have been divided into several sections according to the form of the bloom. Following are the flower-form classifications generally recognized in North America and Europe.

Single

Less spectacular perhaps than the flowers of double form, the singles often have an uncluttered beauty that is classic in its appeal. A single row of petals—anywhere from five to 10 or 12—surrounds a circle of functional, pollen-bearing stamens and carpels. Positioned right in the center of the bloom, the seed-bearing carpels are visible as soon as the flower opens. Species peonies most often produce single flowers.

Examples include 'America', 'Dawn Pink', 'Josette', 'Krinkled White', 'Pico', 'President Lincoln', 'Scarlett O'Hara', 'Sea Shell', 'Spellbinder' and 'White Wings'.

Japanese

Although similar to the singles, in this form the filaments at the center of the flower have broadened slightly and flattened, while the anthers are incomplete, holding no free pollen. This results in the petals remaining free of staining.

In Japanese forms the stamens are in the first stage of doubling. In this changed form they are termed staminodes—finely cut, petal-like segments that keep some yellow pollen color on their tips. The centers may be bright gold, milky white or a lighter or darker shade of the color of the surrounding saucer of petals.

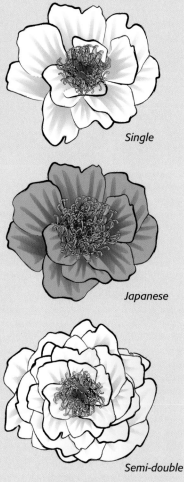

Single

Japanese

Semi-double

Double

Bomb

These tend to be graceful plants that produce lots of blooms on strong stems—stunning as cut flowers and attractive as garden subjects, especially when planted in groups. Some of the taller varieties may need staking, especially where heavy rain comes during the peony-flowering season.

The Japanese people prized the combination of pristine appearance and simplicity of form. Many of the first peonies of this type were imported to the West from Japan.

Examples include 'Nippon Beauty', 'Nippon Brilliant', 'Rosaurea', 'Shaylor's Sunburst', 'Sword Dance' and 'Westerner'.

Anemone

In a genus of showy flowers, these peonies are striking. Similar in appearance to the Japanese-style blooms, they are a step further on the path toward doubling. Each large individual flower forms a small bouquet in its own right, with a saucer of full petals on which sits a fluffy marshmallow of petalodes or staminodes that are further transformed. They no longer resemble the stamens from which they are derived but look more petal-like, though still narrow. They are almost always a single color, either coordinating or contrasting with the color of the guard petals. Frequently they are yellow or white.

Although the anatomy of these and the Japanese form is similar to that of single flowers, their appearance is markedly different.

Examples include 'Bowl of Beauty', 'Break o' Day', 'Do Tell', 'Dragon's Nest', 'Fancy Nancy', 'Gay Paree' and 'Prairie Afire'.

Semi-double

In this form the stamens have transformed even further, creating a profusion of outer petals that gives the effect of an Elizabethan ruff surrounding a distinct center of often bright yellow, pollen-bearing stamens and functional carpels. The yellow coloring of the center is a noticeable feature of this type of flower.

Examples include 'Alexander Woollcott', 'Helen Matthews', 'Lady Alexandra Duff', 'Marie Jacquin', 'Minnie Shaylor', 'Miss America', 'Rare China', 'Red Goddess', 'Silvia Saunders' and 'The Mighty Mo'.

Double

These are blooms for those who love enormous, extravagant flowers filled with masses of petals in textures of Thai silk or watered taffeta. Forget the meaning of life, as in producing offspring. Many of these blooms contain no stamens—they have all been transformed into staminodes or petalodes—and their main purpose is to seduce. Only rarely are the carpels useable for breeding, let alone being visible in the center of the flower.

Sometimes they are described as "two" or even "triple stage double," and in these it seems that the one massive bloom is a composition of several tightly packed flowers, occasionally with a thin ring of natural stamens defining each "flower" or section.

Examples include 'Ann Cousins', 'Festiva Maxima', 'Kansas', 'Karl Rosenfeld', 'Louise Lossing', 'Monsieur Jules Elie', 'Sarah Bernhardt' and 'Shannon'.

Bomb

For show-class purposes, the American Peony Society distinguishes another type of double bloom—called "bomb" (or "double bomb"; also spelled "bombe")—in which there is an outer ring of guard petals that are longer than the transformed petals. They surround the center in these blooms, and both the guard and transformed petals display the same texture and color density. In a well-formed bloom, the central petals form a closely rounded ball when the bud first opens. As the flower matures, it continues to grow larger, eventually forming a substantial mound. Think of a baked Alaska, or bombe Alaska, dessert, presented on an elegant stemmed dish.

Examples include 'Angel Cheeks', 'Bridal Shower', 'Raspberry Sundae' and 'Red Charm'.

ABOVE: 'Red Charm' opens dark crimson and brightens to cerise.

2 The Ancestors—Peony Species

Where did they come from, these sumptuous flowers that have seduced gardeners for centuries and sell in florist shops today for enormous prices?

The answer is complicated. Geographically speaking, the natural habitat of peonies spreads from the Kola Peninsula on the Barents Sea, through the Urals to Siberia; from Tibet and southwestern China to Manchuria and Japan; from France, Spain, Portugal and Switzerland across central and eastern Europe and around the Mediterranean to the Greek Islands, Turkey and on to the Caucasus. A couple of species are endemic to California, but no peony species occurs naturally in the Southern Hemisphere.

They have been found growing on mountainsides in China at more than 9000 ft. (2750 m) above sea level, and on grassy hillsides in southern Spain. They grow on coastal cliffs and at the edges of deciduous forests. Many of the species are rare in the wild; some are at risk of extinction. Five Mediterranean species are protected from collection under the Berne Convention of 1979; others have not been found in the wild for so long that they are considered extinct.

The huge range of opulent blooms available today is the result of sometimes centuries of cross-pollination. At first sight they seem to have little in common with the uncomplicated, single blooms of the species that have long held almost no appeal for gardeners. But peonies are now becoming big news in the gardening world, and as

OPPOSITE: 'Scarlet Emperor'.

RIGHT: Shades of coral, pink and cream make a spectacular arrangement, Keukenhof, the Netherlands.

attention is focused on the beautiful, complicated blooms of the hybrids, so gardeners seek to know more about their origins. Big frilly blooms don't appeal to everyone. The simple flowers of the species, their often interesting foliage and, in many cases, their shorter stature, make them attractive garden plants. Several North American nurseries include species peonies in their lists of available plants or seeds.

In a genus that has seen so much selection and hybridization over the centuries, the question has to be asked, "Where to now?" A true orange peony seems possible and, of course, there remains the elusive dream of a blue peony.

Dr. James Waddick, who with Josef Halda produced a revolutionary reclassification of peony species in 2004, theorizes that several of the species found on the islands and shores of the Mediterranean—such as *Paeonia broteroi, P. clusii, P. coriacea, P. corsica, P. mascula, P. parnassica* and *P. rhodia*—which have rarely been used in peony breeding programs, could be used to produce herbaceous hybrids that would grow well in warm or mild climates like the west coast of North America and some parts of Australia and South Africa.

Since the 1990s, with the dissolution of the Soviet Union and the increasingly open-door policies of China, formerly inaccessible habitats have become more readily able to be explored. "New" peonies are constantly being sought and described. With increased communication between Chinese botanists and those from the West, information about species—some of which have not been recognized before in the West—is more readily shared and debated. The classification of peony species has long been a subject of much discussion and dissent among botanists. It looks set to continue.

The following species' descriptions, which include some subspecies and varieties, have been compiled to give gardeners a comprehensive reference list and include recent updates in the taxonomy of peonies.

Zones mentioned refer to a system of plant-hardiness assessment that has been

BELOW: 'Comtesse de Tudor'.
BELOW RIGHT: Paeonia lutea var. *ludlowii* (syn. *P. delavayi ludlowii*).

accepted as an international standard. Where a zone number has been given, it indicates the coldest areas in which the plant is likely to survive through an average winter. Note that some readers may find the numbers rather conservative. They are an indication only, not a definitive declaration of survival limits.

Tree peony species

Paeonia decomposita (syn. *P. szechuanica*). This elegant tree peony from Szechuan was first recognized as a separate species by Chinese botanists in 1958. Its slender and deeply divided, almost translucent leaves and the satiny sheen of its pink petals distinguish this peony from all others.

ABOVE: 'Plainsman.'

Paeonia delavayi. This name, according to the new *Flora of China*, now includes a group of plants that, over the years, has moved backward and forward between being classified as varying separate species and existing as a group under an umbrella name. What is certain is that the members of this group of plants have many points in common, yet the flowers differ in their color and the way they are presented on the shrub. This group includes, among others, plants that have been called at various times *Paeonia delavayi* var. *alba*; *P. delavayi* var. *angustiloba*; *P. delavayi* var. *atropurpurea*; *P. delavayi* var. *lutea*; *P. lutea*; *P. potaninii*; *P. potaninii* var. *trollioides*; and *P. trollioides*.

These peonies are shrubs of varying heights, some growing as tall as 6 ft. (1.8 m). Flowers may be yellow, yellow with a red or purple-red spot at the base, red, dark red or dark purple-red; they are sometimes white, green-yellow, yellow with a red margin or orange-red. The stamens may also vary in color between yellow, pink, red or dark purple-red. Seedpods have brightly colored sepals and the seeds are large and black. The natural habitat is dry pine or oak woods, thickets or occasionally grassy slopes at 6000–11,000 ft. (1800–3300 m) in western Szechuan, southeastern Tibet and central and northern Yunnan.

The original plants were found by the French missionary priest Père Jean Marie Delavay in the early 1880s, in north Yunnan. Flowers are often small and tend to hang their heads. The variety, formerly named *Paeonia lutea*, has proved valuable because of the genes it has passed on to its descendants, in particular the yellow color that has been bred into many hybrid tree peonies. They are useful plants at the edge of woodland areas, adding interest among other shrubs with their attractive foliage.

Unfortunately, when plants are reclassified we often lose a little bit of their associated history. *Paeonia potaninii* was named in 1921 in memory of an eminent Russian explorer and naturalist, Gregori Potanin, and this variety, unusually, spreads by stolons. The *trollioides* variety bears yellow flowers that are held more erect than those of the other varieties, and they are globe-shaped rather than open-faced.

Paeonia lutea var. *ludlowii* is also included in *P. delavayi* in a recent revision. It

ABOVE: *Paeonia potaninii* var. *trollioides*, from the painting by Lilian Snelling in *Study of the Genus Paeonia* by F.C. Stern.

ABOVE RIGHT: *Paeonia delavayi*.

was originally found in Tibet in 1936 by British plant-hunters Frank Ludlow and George Sherriff and is generally recognized as a more attractive garden subject than *P. lutea*. The plant is robust, with outward-facing flowers that are bigger, brighter and more prolific than those of *P. lutea* and it grows quickly, in the right conditions soon becoming a voluminous small tree. It makes a good specimen plant for large gardens. The large leaves turn bright gold in autumn. *P. lutea* hybrids make good windbreaks in summer as, although deciduous, their foliage goes right to the ground, their roots grow down rather than out, and they are not invasive.

Paeonia delavayi is hardy to zone 5 but will seldom flower below zone 7.

Paeonia jishanensis. Originally thought to be a variety of *P. suffruticosa*, this tree-peony species was first found by British collector William Purdom in the northwest of China in 1910. It grows to about 4 ft. (120 cm) in height and bears single white flowers, each with 10 petals.

Paeonia ostii is a newly described (1992) species of tree peony. It makes an attractive garden plant with big white flowers that are occasionally tinged with pink, and while it may be lanky for the first few years, it will become bushy and rounded as it matures. Attractive gray bark and woody seedpods add another dimension to this plant which grows to 5 ft. (1.5 m) and is hardy to zone 5. It, or a derived cultivar, has been recently imported in large numbers to Europe, often offered under the name Fen(g) Dan Bai, which is a generic cultivar raised for medicinal purposes in China. The somewhat fragile-looking, large (6 in./15 cm) semi-double white blooms appear early in the season and, because of this, can suffer frost damage. The mature stems are silver-gray, with peeling bark.

Paeonia quii is another newly declared species. It is similar to *P. jishanensis*, with slight differences in the foliage.

Paeonia rockii. For a long time this plant, known only in cultivation and assumed to be the species from which all tree peonies were derived, was called *P. suffruticosa*. It was not found in the wild until 1914 and was subsequently renamed *P. rockii*. Chinese botanist Hong De Yuan and his associates stated in 1992 that plants previously designated as *P. suffruticosa* are in fact cultivars developed in China (later in Japan) over a period of centuries and were derived from various crosses between four wild species newly described as *P. ostii*—the wild tree peony that served as a main genetic base for the cultivars; *P. jishanensis* (formerly known as *P. suffruticosa* var. *spontanea*); *P. rockii*; and *P. yananensis*. Hardy to zone 5. *P. suffruticosa* no longer formally exists as a species, though many plants are still described under the name.

Paeonia yananensis. From northwest China, this is one of the tree peony species formerly grouped under the umbrella of *P. suffruticosa*. It grows to 16 in. (40 cm) high, and the attractive white flowers are more fully petalled than many singles. At the base of each petal is a teardrop-shaped blotch in wine-red.

Herbaceous peony species

Paeonia anomala. In its natural habitat this peony grows in conifer woods, on rocky hillsides among shrubs and in dry grasslands from the Kola Peninsula near the Barents Sea, through the Urals of Russia and possibly into northern China. The plant grows 18–22 in. (45–55 cm) tall, with flowers about 2 in. (5 cm) across, usually borne one to a stem. The color range is similar to *P. veitchii*—from pink to deep magenta-red and occasionally white. Among the very earliest of the species to flower, often coming into bloom in mid-spring, this peony has no fragrance. With fernlike, shiny green foliage, it is a hardy plant and easy to grow, tolerating some shade and dry conditions in summer. Seedpods are hairy and the seeds black. Hardy to zone 4.

Paeonia beresowskii. From the western provinces of China near the Tibetan border, *P. beresowskii* was named by a Russian botanist in the 1920s. It is similar to *P. veitchii* but is not available as a garden plant.

Paeonia broteroi. A native of Portugal and Spain, this herbaceous peony has shiny leaves and cup-shaped flowers that are rose-pink with a yellow center. The plant grows to about 15 in. (38 cm). Hardy to zone 6.

Paeonia brownii. This peony was found by plant-hunter David Douglas in the

BELOW: *Paeonia rockii.*

Blue Mountains in Oregon and named by him after the botanist Robert Brown. It is one of only two species native to North America and it was introduced into Europe in 1826. It is a low-growing plant (8–16 in. 20–40 cm) and the more widespread of North America's two peonies, whose nearest relatives are the tree peonies of China. Bowl-shaped flowers of gold, green and maroon, with a golden boss, appear in May to June. *Paeonia brownii* is native to dry sagebrush and Ponderosa-pine country from British Columbia south to Wyoming, Nevada, Utah and northern California. It is often found tucked under bushes in the wild above 3000 ft. (900 m).

Pacific Rim Nursery in Canada reports that *Paeonia brownii* thrives in its nursery in British Columbia in 10 times more rain than the 7–10 in. (18–25 cm) it is used to. Hardy to at least zone 6.

Paeonia californica. The second native North American species, *P. californica* is sometimes considered a subspecies of *P. brownii* but differs from it in being taller at 14–30 in. (35–75 cm) and fuller and more branched, with green sepals and more scarlet in its petals, leaves that are pale on the underside, and longer petals and leaflets with oval rather than round tips.

It is found from Monterey south to San Diego, blooming from January to March in the Northern Hemisphere and going deciduous in May. Flowers are small and maroon in color—about 1 in. (2.5 cm) across—and they hang their heads on stems that range from 6 to 18 in. (15 to 45 cm) in height. The foliage is blue-green. Hardy to possibly zone 6.

Paeonia cambessedesii (syn. *Paeonia corsica*). Native to the Balearic Islands in the western Mediterranean, this peony is endangered owing to coastal development and the fact that the local goats eat the seedheads! One of the smallest species in the genus and one of the least cold-hardy (zone 7 or above), it is distinguished not only by its beautiful mauve-pink flowers, which open to show golden stamens, but also by its thick, lustrous, tri-lobed foliage—dark green on top, deep purple beneath. The multi-carpel seedheads look fantastic with a combination of blue fertile seeds and brilliant scarlet sterile ones.

This peony needs shelter from late spring frosts, requires sharply draining soil and does not like excessive summer moisture. Winter temperatures below about 25°F (−4°C) are usually deleterious to its health. It is a small species, growing to about 18 in. (45 cm) tall and, if you can raise it successfully, will make a good rock-garden plant. It also does well planted among shrubs or against a wall, which will offer it some protection in winter. It is one of the species protected under the Berne Convention.

Paeonia clusii. This hill-dwelling peony is from Crete and Karpathos, where it grows at 3600–4500 ft. (1100–1400 m). When happy, it flowers profusely. The blooms are

OPPOSITE: *Paeonia broteroi.*

poppylike, small, single, perfumed and white, with pale beige stamens. The grayish foliage is fernlike. Given its place of origin, it is not hardy, but would be suitable to grow in warmer climates.

Paeonia coriacea. The name of this peony refers to the leathery texture of its leaves. Its flowers are rose-red and it has been used by hybridizers to produce lavender and light-purple hybrids. It may grow to 40 in. (100 cm) and is a native of Spain, Morocco and Algeria. Hardy to zone 7–8.

Paeonia x *chamaeleon.* This plant is considered a natural hybrid of *P. mlokosewitschii* and *P. caucasica,* but that is still open to debate. It flowers in late spring and grows to 24 in. (60 cm), and the blooms are variable from clone to clone.

Paeonia emodi. Named after the Latin for Himalaya, Emodi Montes, where it grows in forest clearings in the western range at altitudes up to 9600 ft. (2900 m), this peony is very early blooming. The delicately textured, light green foliage can often be damaged by late frosts. It forms a lush plant of shiny cut leaves, growing sometimes to nearly 3 ft. (1 m) in height. The flower is single, icy-white with a ring of golden stamens, and it looks somewhat like the Japanese anemone (*A. hupehensis*). This is one of the few species that produces more than one flower to a stem. The seedpods become a deep red-brown as they mature. *P. emodi* tends to hybridize with other species. Given its origins, it is probably not the best species for gardeners in warm, humid regions. Hardy to zone 6.

Paeonia japonica. This handsome plant with singularly simple white flowers is, as its name suggests, a native of Japan, where it grows in deciduous forests in mountains up to about 4000 ft. (1200 m). As a garden plant growing to 18 in. (45 cm), it is suited to open woodland. Hardy to zone 5.

Paeonia kavachensis. Coming from Russia's Caucasus Mountains, *P. kavachensis* is sometimes called *P. caucasica* or *P. mascula*. Pacific Rim Nursery in British Columbia raised plants from material that the Czech collector Petr Vasak found in 1991 at 150–600 ft. (45–180 m) in the foothills of the western Caucasus, near Sochi, on the Black Sea. It has violet-pink flowers, about 4 in. (10 cm) across, and blooms in late spring. It is a plant of open forest and prefers part-day shade. Height is about 20 in. (50 cm), and it is hardy to at least zone 6.

Paeonia kesrouanensis. This peony is a native of Syria, Lebanon and Turkey and is hard to distinguish from *P. mascula* (see page 33).

Paeonia lactiflora (syn. *P. edulis*, *P. albiflora*, *P. chinensis*, *P. sinensis*). This tough species will thrive in heavier soils than those peonies coming from the Mediterranean areas. A native of northern China, Siberia, Mongolia and parts of Tibet, it grows on open stony slopes, riverbanks and sparse woodland edges and will tolerate bitterly cold temperatures—as low as −45°F (−50°C). It is an ornamental and long-lived plant, known to have survived in gardens for more than 50 years and growing to about 3 ft. (1 m) in height. The elegantly simple blooms are scented and silky white, faintly flushed with pink and crowned in the center with pale golden stamens, though there are also pink and red forms.

BELOW: **Paeonia cambessedesii**, from the painting by Lilian Snelling in *Study of the Genus Paeonia* by F.C. Stern.

This peony is the ancestor of most modern herbaceous hybrids. Its progeny are known as Chinese peonies, and the Chinese had already worked with *Paeonia lactiflora* to produce hundreds of distinctive forms even before its introduction to the West in the late 18th century. Following its arrival in Britain, a new rush of hybridization ensued and the elaborate showpiece varieties that were a feature of Victorian and Edwardian gardens, with blooms that range from clear white through pink and deepest crimson, have the genes of *Paeonia lactiflora* in their pedigrees. *P. lactiflora* introduced perfume into many of its hybrids, plus the ability to bear more than one flower per stem, and the offspring also have inherited the later flowering season of the parent plant, blooming in early summer.

An easily grown and undemanding plant, *P. lactiflora* will grow in a variety of soils, though it will not survive in waterlogged conditions or drought. It does best in a deep, rich soil, preferably neutral or slightly alkaline, growing equally well in sun

or light shade, so long as it has moisture in summer. This species is lime-tolerant. Plants grown on sandy soils tend to produce more leaves and fewer flowers; those growing on clay take longer to become established but produce better blooms.

P. lactiflora has been used in Chinese herbal medicine for more than 1500 years. The roots are harvested in the autumn from cultivated plants that are four to five years old and are boiled before being sun-dried for later use. When the whole root is harvested it is called "Chi shaoyao" and is used to purify the blood and relieve pain. If the bark is removed during preparation, then it is called "Bai shaoyao" and is believed to nourish the blood also. Hardy to zone 2.

Paeonia lagodechiana. This peony is sometimes referred to as the "Lagodechi Gorge peony," from its only known natural habitat in Georgia's Caucasus Mountains, where it grows in open woodland; in the garden it prefers some shade. Large pink flowers with purple filaments and orange anthers bloom in mid-spring above glaucous leaves. It grows to a maximum height of about 40 in. (100 cm). Hardy to zone 6.

OPPOSITE: 'Orange Cup'.
ABOVE *Paeonia mascula* ssp. *mascula.*

Paeonia macrophylla. This peony is extremely rare in cultivation. Martin Page of the American Peony Society reports that this species, a native of a small area in Georgia, in the former Soviet Union, where it occurs in mountain forests at altitudes of between 2600 and 3300 ft. (800 and 1000 m), was first described in 1895 as *P. wittmanniana* var. *macrophylla.* The two are similar but, as its name suggests, *P. macrophylla* has massive leaves that evidently can reach 9.5 in. (24 cm) long by 6 in. (15 cm) wide. They are shiny on the upper surface and have deeply depressed veins that give them a distinctive blistered appearance.

The solitary flowers of *P. macrophylla,* appearing in mid-spring, seem pale yellow in bud, but open ivory-white with the merest hint of yellow. There is a slight tinge of magenta at the base of the petals, which fades after a couple of days. They measure up to 3 in. (7.5 cm) across.

When the seedpods open they are extremely colorful, with the fertile seeds a rich blue-black color, and the infertile ovules a vivid rose-red. The leaves have a pungent, acrid smell, particularly conspicuous when the plant is flowering, which is enough to separate it from other species of peony. It can be distinguished from *P. wittmanniana* by the distinctive appearance of its leaves. Hardy to zone 7.

Paeonia mairei. A native of mountains in the west of China, this species is not known in cultivation. A low-growing peony, about 18 in. (45 cm) high, it has rose-pink flowers in late spring to early summer. Hardy to zone 6.

Paeonia mascula. Also known as "the male peony," this species comes from around the Mediterranean and Turkey and thrives in open rocky limestone slopes or in areas of scrub or light woodland. Growing about 3 ft. (1 m) tall, it is one of the

earliest introductions into Britain. It may have arrived as early as 1299 from southern Europe, possibly brought with the Augustinian monks and planted on the tiny island of Steep Holme in the Bristol Channel when they settled there. Here these peonies still thrive, happily naturalized among the undergrowth, the only place in the U.K. where peonies still grow wild.

Paeonia mascula likes well-drained soil and full sun, and is early to bloom. The large, single flowers have stamens tipped with gold and range in color through soft pink to violet-rose, though often they are a deep crimson-purple. The foliage is an attractive glossy dark green. In autumn the seedpods open, showing rose-red seeds, similar to coral, which give the plant its other name of *P. corallina*. Plants grow to about 24 in. (60 cm).

During monastic times this plant no doubt was valued for its medicinal properties. John Parkinson, gardener to Charles I of England, writes about it in his *Paradisus in Sole*, saying that "we cherish them for their beauty and delight of their goodly flowers as well as for their physical virtues." Hardy to zone 4.

P. mascula ssp. *arietina*. This peony from eastern Europe, Turkey and Syria has semi-double blooms of a pinky-red that open widely to show bosses of red filaments topped by creamy anthers. It differs from *P. mascula* in the hairiness of the undersides of its leaves. The name "arietina" means ramlike and describes the shape of the plant's fruit.

P. mascula ssp. *hellenica* has pinky-white blooms flushed crimson at the base.

P. mascula ssp. *triternata* (syn. *P. daurica*) is a native of Ukraine and countries farther south such as Turkey and Romania. The flowers are pink shading to magenta, single, with a yellow center, and they appear in early summer. The plant grows about 20 in. (50 cm) tall and is happy in full sun or partial shade. The seedpods open to reveal bright red infertile ovules and fertile blue-black rounded seeds.

Paeonia mlokosewitschii. Otherwise known as "Molly-the-witch," this is another species from the Caucasus, where it grows on rocky, sunny slopes and in oak or beech forests. It is well known in gardens for its early though short-lived flowers usually ivory through to yellow, cup-shaped and single, one per stem. However, plants in cultivation can also produce flowers in a wide range of pinks, bronzes and almost white, and a pink flush on the flowers is typical of this variable species. Some plants produced under this name turn out to be hybrids. Its stems are burgundy tinted and the bush grows to about 2 ft. (60 cm) tall.

Christopher Lloyd, of English gardening renown, has commented that "it flowers for about five days in early May, and is at its ravishing best for about four hours in the middle of this period." Don't be deterred by such waspish comment. Gorgeous

TOP: 'Coral Fay'.
MIDDLE: 'Late Windflower.'
ABOVE: 'Flame', early to mid-season.

ABOVE: *Paeonia mlokosewitschii.*

crimson shoots start appearing above ground in late winter. The witch's cloak of wide, almost rounded leaves in an attractive gray-green color is lovely throughout summer, and just wait for late summer when her pods open to expose wickedly black and infertile red seeds. Hardy to zone 6.

Paeonia mollis. This peony is a rare or possibly extinct plant in the wild. It was taken to the U.K. in the 19th century from its native Siberia. An early-blooming species, it has single, usually crimson, sometimes rosy-pink and occasionally white cupped flowers held well above the bush. The plant grows to about 24 in. (60 cm) tall. As you would expect, given its natural home, it is extremely hardy, a quality that has been passed on to some modern hybrids with *P. mollis* parentage.

Available from some U.S. nurseries, *Paeonia mollis* is an attractive plant in the garden, good for growing at the edge of woodland areas where there is little competition from other roots. Hardy to zone 4.

Paeonia obovata. With large, oval, light green leaves and goblet-shaped flowers that are mauve-purple, this peony is native to Siberia, Manchuria, China, Korea and Japan, and was collected by E.H. Wilson in 1900. As the name suggests, the flowers are smoothly oval like an egg. The plant grows to 28 in. (70 cm) tall and is hardy to zone 4.

P. obovata 'Alba', a well-known garden plant, and *P. obovata* 'Willmottiae' both have white flowers.

ABOVE: 'Cytherea',
P. lactiflora x P. peregrina.

ABOVE RIGHT: Paeonia officinalis 'Rubra Plena'.

Paeonia officinalis. Formerly known also as "the female peony," this peony appears in writings as early as 370 BC, when Theophrastus, philosopher and colleague of Aristotle, and a practical gardener, whom some call "the father of botany," mentions it in his *Enquiry into Plants.* He recommended it for healing wounds.

With single crimson flowers about 5 in. (12 cm) across that are highlighted by a ring of golden stamens, this plant is a native of the Mediterranean, where it grows in meadows, bushy areas and grassy scrub. It flowers early in the season, likes partial shade, has attractive foliage, may grow to 3 ft. (1 m) tall and does not require staking.

It is not known exactly when the first plants of the double form reached Britain from the eastern Mediterranean, but Gerard includes an illustration of the double white peony in his *Herbal*, published in 1597.

Paeonia officinalis 'Rubra Plena' has been a favorite in gardens for generations and has double flowers in a rich crimson shade. "No flower that I know so faire, great and double," wrote herbalist John Parkinson in 1629 about this luscious crimson beauty. If someone can recognize only one peony, it will most likely be this one. A favorite in cottage gardens for centuries, it is still a popular plant among peony growers. Its flowering season is early but short, though the blooms are produced successively and make good cut flowers. The huge, bright green, deeply cut leaves are attractive all summer. The plants are large—about 2 ft. (60 cm) tall—and they like rich, well-drained soil. Though they are happy in full sun, they will also tolerate light shade, in which position the flowers last longer.

'Rosea Plena' produces a double rose bloom, and 'Alba Plena' opens flesh-pink and fades to an uninteresting cream. All three have an unpleasant odour.

Paeonia officinalis ssp. *banatica* is one of the larger subspecies with bowl-shaped, red flowers up to 5½ in. (14 cm) across. It was first discovered in Romania and is also found in Hungary and Serbia.

Paeonia officinalis ssp. *humilis* (formerly *P. humilis* or *P. officinalis* ssp. *macrocarpa*) is a native of Spain and southern France. Flowers are purple-red, measure up to 5 in. (12 cm) across and appear in late spring to early summer.

Paeonia officinalis ssp. *villosa* varies little from *P.o.* ssp. *humilis* but is native to southern France and central Italy. Hardy to zone 4.

Paeonia parnassica is native to the mountains of central Greece and grows about 25 in. (65 cm) high. The large flowers—up to 5 in. (12 cm) wide—are deep purple-red and appear in late spring. This plant is increasingly rare in its native habitat and is protected under the Berne Convention. Hardy to zone 8.

Paeonia peregrina is also sometimes known as the "Constantinople peony" and still grows wild among scrub in Romania, Greece and Turkey. This is the species used by propagators to produce the true red, coral, salmon and cherry-pink hybrids. A beautiful garden plant, growing to about 3 ft. (1 m), it has very finely dissected leaves and single, cup-shaped blooms of glistening red with a ring of bright golden anthers and glossy, deep green foliage. It likes good drainage and sandy rather than heavy soil. This species was known to English gardeners of the 17th century. Parkinson, in his writings, referred to it as being "the color of the tulip." Hardy to zone 4.

Paeonia ruprechtiana. This herbaceous peony, rarely seen in gardens, grows to about 20 in. (50 cm) tall. It is early-flowering and has large violet-red blooms and shiny leaves that are divided into threes, with rounded leaflets. Its foliage resembles *P. caucasica* in some respects; but the leaves of *Paeonia ruprechtiana* are almost hairless on the underside, while those of *P. caucasica* are hairy. Named for the Russian botanist Franz Josef Ivanovich Ruprecht (d. 1870), it is native to the western Caucasus Mountains and is hardy to zone 6.

ABOVE: *Paeonia peregrina.*

Paeonia sinjiangensis is very similar to both *P. anomala* and *P. veitchii* and is classified by some botanists as a synonym for the latter. It is a native of the province of Xinjiang and may grow to 30 in. (75 cm).

Paeonia sterniana is similar to *P. emodi*. Its natural habitat is the Tsangpo Valley in eastern Tibet, where it grows to 36 in. (90 cm) tall at an altitude of 9500 ft. (2900 m). Its flowers, borne only one per stem, are single and white. It is difficult to obtain as a garden plant. Hardy to zone 4.

Paeonia tenuifolia is native in areas from southeastern Europe east to the Caucasus, found on dry grasslands and in open woodland. Some enthusiasts believe it grows best in gardens where winters are cold, with reliable snow cover, and it is one of the first peonies to bloom each season. The flowers, one per stem, are dark crimson-red and single, with golden stamens, usually about 4 in. (10 cm) across.

P. tenuifolia, or the so-called fern-leaf peony, is probably the most frequently mentioned rock-garden peony, and it is a favorite with gardeners because of its attractive foliage—almost grasslike in its delicacy—which shows off the single blooms to advantage. Hardy to zone 4.

There are several *Paeonia tenuifolia* hybrids—'Little Red Gem', 'Early Scout' (a profuse bloomer), 'Windchimes', 'Laddie', 'Smouthi', 'Merry Mayshine'—that are all well-suited to rock gardens. Because of their delicate form and low-growing habit, they look great alongside many alpines. The hybrids have finely dissected foliage, similar to that of the parent, and the flowers are also single and red, some having a pleasant fragrance. They range in height from 12–24 in. (30–60 cm). A form with double flowers, *Paeonia tenuifolia* 'Plena', sometimes called "the Adonis peony," is common in cultivation, though not always easy to maintain.

Paeonia tenuifolia ssp. *lithophila* is sometimes known simply as *P. lithophila*. Native to the eastern Crimea, it is similar to *P. tenuifolia*, but smaller, with the leaves more finely cut. The flowers are blood-red with golden filaments and anthers, and they are very early blooming. Height is about 12 in. (30 cm). Hardy to at least zone 6.

Paeonia veitchii is native to alpine meadows, scrub and mountain steppes in northwest China at altitudes to 12,000 ft. (3600 m). The flowers, about 2 in. (5 cm) across, resemble dainty nodding poppies and are evenly distributed over the bush. With more than one bloom per stem, in shades of pink through magenta, or occasionally white, they have an extended flowering period but no noticeable perfume. Flowering begins about three weeks before the *Paeonia lactiflora* cultivars, but there is also a late-blooming form.

The bush itself is attractive because of the deeply cut, dark green foliage, and in autumn the seedpods, which are sometimes tinged with red, add to the seasonal interest. Quite hardy and easy to grow (to about 20 in. or 50 cm), happy in full sun or half-shade, this species is suitable for the back of a rock garden, as a mid-height plant in a border, or on the edge of a woodland area.

Paeonia veitchii 'Woodwardii' is a similar plant but attains only about half the height. Flowers are deep pink and single, and will cross with *P. emodi* to produce seedlings that are taller than the parents, with single blooms ranging from white to deep pink. Hardy to zone 4.

Paeonia wittmanniana, a rare species coming from the northwest Caucasus, is a close relation of *P. mlokosewitschii*. It has delicate creamy-yellow single flowers, cup-shaped and adorned with gold-tipped stamens that go on to produce bright, coral-red seeds. Blooming early in spring, this peony, like most of the species from the Caucasus, will tolerate some shade. When crossed with *P. lactiflora* varieties, many of the resulting hybrids are early flowering, with large, fragrant single blooms that last well in the vase.

BELOW: Paeonia tenuifolia.

3 The Eternal Allure of the Peony

Humans respond instinctively to beauty, even though our perception of what is beautiful is most often the result of cultural conditioning. However, I believe our response to the beauty (or otherwise) of flowers usually comes from deep within the individual psyche. If this is true, there is something about a peony flower that has universal appeal. Though fashions come and go in the short term, peonies, like lilies, roses and irises, have been admired and sought after through countless ages, by people of many cultures, of all persuasions, old or young, rich or poor. Poets have praised them. Horticulturists have hybridized them. They appear in paintings and they exist in gardens in every corner of the globe where the climate is suitable.

Peonies as medicine

Curiously though, this highly decorative plant was once treasured more for its roots than for its flowers. In the time of Hippocrates, 400 years before the birth of Christ, the peony was used to treat epilepsy. The plant was named after Paeon, physician to the gods in ancient Greek times. He reputedly used the sap from the roots to cure a wartime wound suffered by Pluto. In the way of those ancient gods, Paeon's mentor Aesculapius became jealous of the physician's success

OPPOSITE: Cool, sophisticated beauty: 'Garden Peace'.

RIGHT: 'Lonesome Dove' showing the typical faint pink blush on its bud.

and arranged to have him killed. But Pluto hadn't forgotten that he owed his life to Paeon. To save him from the wrath of Aesculapius, he turned Paeon into the flower that has borne his name ever since. Paeon was worshipped as a god of healing, and a hymn in his praise became known as a paean. Since then many a paean has been written to peonies.

The peony root's reputation for healing followed it through the centuries, endowing it with almost magical properties. The plant is mentioned at length in *A Modern Herbal* by Mrs. M. Grieve, along with all the folklore that attached itself to the plant over time. She gives detailed directions for preparing the root and states that it was formerly used successfully in the treatment of convulsions, epilepsy and lunacy. An infusion of the powdered root was recommended for obstructions of the liver, and even the seeds were considered important. Those who feared evil spirits strung these as a necklace and wore it as a charm; in the medieval Arab world, a similar necklace was recommended as a treatment against epilepsy.

Paeonia officinalis, whose root was so important in early medicine, is a herbaceous species that is native to many European countries and exists in both a double red and a white form. Although it is not known when this plant was introduced into England, it was initially found in monasteries and known as the "Benedictine Rose." There is evidence to show that the monk in charge of the infirmary of Durham Priory bought 3 pounds (1.3 kg) of the seed of the crimson-flowered variety in 1299, when it was used to stave off nightmares and to help with pain relief.

In medieval England, the roots of *Paeonia officinalis* were reputed to be used by the very rich as an accompaniment to pork dishes, roasted presumably. Poor people could afford to use it only as a seasoning. The seeds were ground and, along with pepper, salt, garlic and other herbs and spices, used as a flavouring for soups. The Alewife, in the vision of Piers Plowman, from the allegorical narrative written in the 14th century, says, "I have pepper and peony seed and a pound of garlic and a farthing worth of fennel seed for fasting days."

The so-called white peony, a herbaceous species with stunning double flowers, did not arrive in Britain until 1784. Confusingly it is known by several names, among them *Paeonia albiflora, P. edulis* and *P. lactiflora*. The last is now generally accepted as its correct name. It was developed early as a garden flower in China and came to Europe in the latter part of the 18th century after a Russian traveler discovered it growing in Siberia. It is said that the Mongols also enjoyed peony soup, but they boiled the roots in the soup and ground the seeds to add to their tea—hence, the alternative botanical name of *P. edulis*. This plant still graces the Old Imperial Summer Palace near Beijing.

Paeonia officinalis is only rarely prescribed nowadays in European medicine, but the medicinal use of peonies in China goes back at least 1500 years and continues today. The roots, bark, seeds and flowers of several species all have their part to play in traditional Chinese medicine.

BELOW: 'Red Charm' first appeared in the United States in 1944 and has been consistently popular ever since, especially as a cut flower.

"Mu dan pi," made from the bark of the roots of tree peonies, is said to "cool the blood" and additionally is reputed to have antibacterial properties. The peony root sold as a herbal remedy, usually *Paeonia lactiflora*, is harvested in late summer or early autumn and cleaned. The lateral roots and skin are removed, it may be boiled lightly, and then the root is dried. Known as "Chi shao yao," or "Bai shao yao" when the bark has been removed, it is used as a more general remedy. As well as cooling blood, it is used to relieve pain and to nourish the blood, and is one of the herb ingredients in "Four Things Soup," a woman's tonic. More specifically it is used to treat gynecological problems, including cramps and excessive bleeding. Because of its antispasmodic properties, it is also prescribed in Chinese medicine for griping abdominal pain, muscle cramps, headaches, ringing in the ears, dizziness and blurred vision. Ancient wisdom claims that women who take the herb on a regular basis become as radiant as the flower itself.

Not only women can benefit from its properties—I have seen peony root recommended for men who wish to remain youthful looking. (Just why its anti-aging effects should be beneficial specifically for men was not enunciated.)

Peony flowers also have their place in herbal medicine. A tea made from the dried crushed petals of various peony species has been used in the past as a cough remedy and as a treatment for hemorrhoids and varicose veins.

Peonies grown for medical use today come mainly from China, Korea and Taiwan, and the bark of their roots is exported throughout Asia for use as an antispasmodic. International medical research suggests that peonies contain chemical compounds that could become useful in the future to treat serious diseases. Should all the claims made for the benefits of peony-based medicine be proved correct, these plants would indeed become a wonder drug.

Ornamental peonies in Asia
China's "King of Flowers"

Although the peony was first cultivated for its medicinal value—the word "shao yao" (or "sho yao") means medicinal herb plant—growers were not slow to appreciate the beauty of its flowers. The herbaceous variety grew wild in much of northern and central China and, as early as AD 536, a Chinese writer describes both red and white peonies, long before they became current in the West. But it is the tree peony—"mudan," or "mou tan"—which came to be called the "King of Flowers" in China and is still regarded as such. Since the first mention of these extravagantly flowering shrubs in the first century AD, peonies have occupied an important place in the medicine, history, art and gardens of the Chinese. During the time of Emperor Yang (605–618) of the Sui Dynasty, 20 cases of tree peonies reportedly were presented to him as tribute, a measure of their commercial value. So valuable did the plants become that connoisseurs paid huge prices for selected varieties, and peonies even featured in dowry settlements.

Later a legend grew up around the peony which added to its popularity. It concerns Wu Zetian, a ruthless royal concubine who eventually engineered her accession to the Imperial throne at the end of the seventh century and became accustomed to getting her own way. One winter's evening in the town of Chang'an, seat of the Imperial family at the time, the imperious empress was feeling somewhat bored and out of sorts. As a diversion she ordered the hundreds of flowers in her palace garden to bloom simultaneously. Next morning she walked down to her palace gardens, impatient to see the results of her decree. Without question, all had obeyed—all, that is, except the stubborn peony. In a fit of rage, the empress banished the peony to Luoyang. Not long after, the court moved its capital to Luoyang, and the peony became the favored flower of the city—as it still is today.

The rulers of the Sui and Tang dynasties brought a measure of stability to China, which in turn brought increased prosperity, more leisure and consequently a flowering of the arts. Beautiful lustrous silk produced during the Tang Dynasty was richly decorated, incorporating stylized patterns of birds, beasts and plants. Peonies appeared frequently as a design motif on silk, on woodcuts or on ceramics. Peonies came to represent spring, and poets used the flower as an allusion to love and the freshness of spring. People became interested not only in growing flowers but also in arranging them. Flower books from the time show us what class flowers belong in and how they characterize different aspects of life. Lwo Chiou presented the nine principles for arranging the peony, the dynasty's national flower.

Unlike trends today that come and go with dizzying speed, the fashion for tree peonies in China was longlasting. During the 250 years of the Tang Dynasty, when the moutan was honored with the title "National Beauty and Heavenly Fragrance" as well as "King of Flowers," and right up until the end of the subsequent Song Dynasty (1279), the tree peony enjoyed enormous prestige.

As people fell under the spell of the tree peony, its culture became an obsession—particularly in the city of Luoyang, which, according to a contemporary observer, "went berserk" during the peony season. Poets and musicians sang the praises of peonies, artists painted them and writers wrote articles about them.

In the *Report on the Luoyang Peonies*, written by a high-ranking civil servant called Ouyang Hsiu (1007–1072), who must also have been a horticulturist of note, the author records more than 90 kinds of tree peonies as well as detailing the gardening techniques of the time. Double flowers with as many petals as possible appealed most to the Chinese, who gave their favorite blooms poetic names such as "Cranes in Red Harmony," "Dancing Green Lion," or "Red of the Morning Cloud." It is thought that the grafting of tree peonies first took place somewhere about this period. Some of Ouyang's cultivars still exist today and are cherished by flower lovers in China and in other countries.

The fortunes of the tree peony fluctuated through the centuries as the fortunes of China itself fluctuated. During the rule of the Mongols in the 13th and 14th

centuries, the culture of tree peonies waned; many varieties were lost. However, with the rise of the later Chinese dynasties the tree peony once again became an important feature of national life. An increasing number of cities throughout the country devoted space and resources to developing varieties of the gorgeous flowers. They proliferated as garden plants and featured in festivals.

We tend to think that throwaway potted plants are a feature of modern life, but in the 1840s the famous English plant-seeker, Robert Fortune, on the hunt for peonies in China, saw tree peonies being shipped from mountain areas where they grew happily, to Canton and other warm places in the south where the climate does not encourage their cultivation. The plants were packed in baskets, without soil, just as the flower buds were forming. Arriving at their destination, they were potted up and sold; the flowers were enjoyed for the season, and then the plants were thrown out. And forget fast courier services. The plants must have taken days, if not weeks, to reach their destination—a measure of the hardiness of the tree peony.

With the downfall of the Qing Dynasty in 1911, however, years of civil disorder and natural disasters combined to drastically reduce the number of tree peony varieties grown in China. Disastrous flooding on the Yellow River in 1933 drowned half the peony fields in Heze, an important center for their cultivation since the 1400s. Starvation followed the floods, and many of the remaining peony fields were dug over and planted with food crops.

After a brief revival in interest following the Communist takeover in 1949, the growing of flowers as ornamentals was forbidden during the 10 years of the Cultural Revolution, from 1966 to 1976, and peonies were supposed to be grown only for medicinal use.

Now, once again, the culture of tree peonies is encouraged in China. National and local governments have invested funds to support research, planting and development of new varieties. It is estimated that there are now over a thousand different cultivars of tree peonies in China.

This flower, which has always represented elegance and poise for the Chinese, is once again an important feature in the calendar of the old Imperial capital of Luoyang—and an important part of the city's economy. So many peonies grow in and around Luoyang that in spring the whole city is redolent with their perfume. In 1982 an annual peony festival, including lantern shows and other forms of entertainment, was inaugurated. During the festival, people come from afar to admire the peonies and enjoy the spectacle of color. In April the streets are festooned with peonies and crowds wander in Peony Square and Peony Park. But the most famous place to view and admire the peonies is Wangcheng Park, the largest park in Luoyang, which includes a zoo, peony gardens, swimming pools and an underground exhibition room of the Han Tomb. In the peony fields on both sides of the Jian River, the focus of the festival, rows of peonies stretch, seemingly

OPPOSITE: Tree peonies in shades of rich crimson.

forever. Thousands of plants, including nearly 400 varieties, grow in just one of the Luoyang peony gardens.

Luoyang is rivaled by the old peony-growing town of Heze, which claims to be the biggest producer of peonies, including tree peonies and the herbaceous varieties, in China. At its annual festival more than 600 cultivars are on display. A peony research institute is based there, and peonies are exported from the city to both domestic and foreign markets.

In the Shanghai Botanical Garden the peony collection includes more than seven thousand plants.

Near the end of the Qing Dynasty, in 1903, the tree peony was named China's national flower, but its reign was short-lived, replaced by the blossom of the plum tree by governmental decree in 1929. In the turmoil of the following decades, the idea of a national flower lapsed, but the age-old Chinese love affair with peonies continues. In 1994 the government set out to once again nominate a national flower for the whole country. Surveys were carried out, and the tree peony received the highest number of votes. For some reason, the government failed to make a decision and people are still waiting for a national flower to be announced.

Japanese developments

Peonies are also highly ranked in Japan. It is thought both herbaceous and tree peonies were introduced into the country from China by itinerant Buddhist monks, about the seventh century. The Chinese name for tree peonies, "moutan," changed to "botan," and they quickly became great favorites, not only for their medicinal value but also for their beauty. The most important flowers of the summer were the iris, lotus and wisteria, and very soon the tree peony enjoyed the same status as these other three. It was often called the "Flower of Prosperity" and occasionally the "Plant of Twenty Days." Along with the cherry and the lotus, it was accorded royal rank, being regarded as "Queen of all flowering plants."

As in China, the peony became a motif often used in Japanese art. Many-petalled, stylized versions of the flower appear on silk panels, on carved ornaments and on elaborate kimonos.

No sooner had peonies arrived than Japanese horticulturists started tinkering with the flowers, seeking to breed flower forms that suited the less flamboyant expression of Japanese style. The blooms gradually produced in Japan were simpler and less complicated than the Chinese varieties. Ito Ifui, a Japanese gardener in the early years of the 18th century, left explicit written information about the culture and propagation of the botan.

The Japanese today still prefer single varieties or semi-double flowers. In addition, they have produced the "Japanese" herbaceous peony, sometimes called the "Imperial" peony, which is recognized as a separate class of bloom. The flower comprises an outer guard ring of petals, either single or double, with the center

OPPOSITE: 'Karen Gray'.

BELOW: 'Hanakisoi', a stunning Japanese tree peony.

consisting of a mound of closely packed, slivered petals, known as staminodes or petalodes. These can be the same color as the guard petals or of a contrasting color. The effect is like a small bouquet of flowers all in one. When the petalodes almost fill the flower it is referred to as an "anemone" peony. (See pages 19–20 for fuller explanation of these forms.)

In 1948 an exciting breakthrough occurred in peony breeding. For many years, enthusiasts had dreamed of crossing a tree peony with a herbaceous variety. Toichi Itoh finally succeeded, and while he did not live to see his hybrids flower, he laid the foundations of a new race of peonies known as "intersectional hybrids."

Interestingly, the peony was not included in the landscaping of Japanese gardens. With the exalted status it had been accorded, it remained for a long time as something to be treated with special attention. Often it was grown in beds reserved for itself, or in large pots. A potted peony might be brought indoors, given a place of special importance and there revered, much in the same way as an opening Higo iris would become the subject of meditation. "Peony gazing" took place in spring, when myriad peony blooms were displayed together and ladies would sit quietly contemplating their beauty.

Today the peony gazing is done mainly in numerous botan parks and public gardens where colorful peony displays are a feature of spring. In *Peonies: The Imperial Flower* (1999), Jane Fearnley-Whittingstall relates that peonies also feature in the annual Shinto religious festival of Bommatsuri, where people come at night to pay their respects to the spirits of their ancestors. The processional route is lit with peony lanterns made from paper or silk, each hung on the end of a long pole.

The Japanese have a fine reputation for their grafting skills and, with a large percentage of the world's tree peonies originating in Japan, peonies have become big business. The country is a major producer of peonies, both herbaceous and tree varieties.

Ornamental peonies in the West

In the United Kingdom

The range of peonies known to have been grown in England up until the 19th century was limited. Both *Paeonia officinalis* and *P. mascula*, growing in monastery gardens, were recorded as early as the 12th century, and a writer of the time, describing the flowers suitable in a garden for the nobility, includes a peony. A woodcut that appeared three centuries later depicts a somewhat stylized but definitely recognizable trio of peonies. Peonies have never featured in European art to the same extent as they have in Asia, but a few botanical paintings of the flowers exist dating from the 17th and 18th centuries.

Although both *Paeonia lactiflora* and a tree peony specimen had arrived in Britain during the latter years of the 18th century, and it is probable that the species *Paeonia tenuifolia*, *P. peregrina* and *P. anomala* were also cultivated then, it was another 50 years before interest in exotic varieties of peonies really grew. It took a combination of factors. The Victorian Age was a time of great curiosity. China and Japan became accessible to Westerners, if reluctantly on the part of their rulers. Adventurers exploring in both countries sent back exotic plants, including varieties of peonies that excited the interest of growers. This coincided with the rise of a middle class with disposable income at a time when it was considered the height

BELOW LEFT: 'Sister Margaret'.
BELOW: 'Roselette's Child'.

of fashion to cultivate unusual or beautiful plants in private gardens. In the days when garden labor was cheap and easy to come by, the large country estates of the aristocracy, or those established by wealthy industrialists, offered plenty of scope for growing large numbers of peonies.

Possibly the first named *Paeonia lactiflora* cultivar to be offered to the general public, in 1808, was 'Whitleyi', a single white bloom named after the nurseryman who first acquired it. 'Whitleyi Major' is still available today and is recognized as being one of the finest single white blooms. Another early herbaceous variety was 'Pottsii'. It was collected in China in 1821 by John Potts, who was seeking plants for the British Horticultural Society.

About 1850 John Salter saw a market opportunity and set out to plant varieties of *Paeonia lactiflora* that other Englishmen had brought from China. James Kelway entered the game in 1864, at first concentrating on improving existing *P. officinalis* types, but it was not long before he started growing peonies on an extensive scale. For the next 40 years he was the dominant peony producer in Britain. By 1885 he was able to catalogue 250 varieties, of which more than 100 were new cultivars he had bred himself. At the beginning of the 20th century, Kelway and Son of Langport, Somerset, was the biggest nursery in Britain. The company's breeding of peonies continued into the middle years of the century with the work of the founder's grandson, also James.

The name Kelway lives on as the developer of many successful varieties that are still available today. 'Kelway's Glorious', bred in 1909, is a good example. A ruffled double white perfumed peony flowering mid- to late season, it is still quoted in lists of exceptional plants and is popular in the United States as one of the peonies that can be grown successfully in the southern states. 'Baroness Schroeder', even older (1889), is another of Kelway's hybrids that is still sought after today.

In France

Peonies in the 19th century made a greater impact across the channel than in England, and the most famous growers and breeders of this era came from France. It is interesting to note that numerous cultivars produced in France during this time are still recognized as superb flowers and are available more than 150 years later.

Early in the 19th century, in the country that had ostensibly abolished royalty, it was due to royal interest in this "king of flowers" that peonies became a feature of French life. Although the Empress Josephine's garden at Malmaison, on the outskirts of Paris, was better known for its collection of roses, it also contained peonies. One, *Paeonia daurica*, now known as *P. mascula* ssp. *triternata* and a native of Siberia, was evidently brought to her in 1810, via England, and was regarded as a rare plant. *Paeonia lactiflora*, with a double white flower, also existed in the garden at Malmaison at this time. A painting by Redouté of *Paeonia suffruticosa* is assumed to have been painted at Malmaison.

Varieties still on the market today originated in the garden of King Louis-Philippe at Neuilly, in the years between 1830 and 1848. It is thought that several growers in the early years of the 19th century were developing seedlings of *P. officinalis*, and by the 1850s Charles Verdier, in Paris, was offering over 50 named varieties in his catalogue.

BELOW: 'Ellen Cowley', early.

Perhaps the first man in Europe to raise peonies from seed, name them and sell the best varieties was M. Nicolas Lemon in Paris during the 1820s. He produced 'Edulis Superba' in 1824, and now, over 175 years later, it is still considered a desirable garden plant. A double pink *P. lactiflora* hybrid that makes a superb cut flower, it has a strong perfume, as do many of Lemon's varieties.

By 1835 Modeste Guérin was producing named Chinese or *Paeonia lactiflora* cultivars that inherited their parents' free-flowering habit and perfume, both of which added enormously to their general appeal. For the next 30 years he worked

at improving this type of peony—by selecting choice seedlings—and introduced more than 40 new varieties, including 'Duchesse d'Orléans', a pink that makes a good cut flower, and 'Modeste Guérin', a double pink, both of which are available today.

The names of several French breeders working later in the century have become almost synonymous with the word peony. Sometimes the passion and the expertise were passed down through family members; at other times the collections of peonies themselves moved from breeder to breeder. The accumulation of plants by the Comte de Cussy—started from peonies he imported from China—passed from his hands to those of Jacques Calot of Douai. For 22 years, from 1850, working with the count's collection, Calot developed a number of new plants. Many of these are prized today in gardens, including the legendary 'Duchesse de Nemours', a beautiful double white that featured in a Monet painting entitled *Spring Flowers*.

In 1872 the enhanced collection once again changed hands, this time passing to M. Félix Crousse, who further fine-tuned selection techniques to produce some plants with seemingly eternal appeal. 'Madame de Verneville', double white, fragrant and early-flowering, is one. 'Félix Crousse', developed in 1885, is another. Appearing in mid- to late season, this peony has double blooms of a rich carmine pink that make good cut flowers.

In 1898 this collection, which already had gained historic importance, passed to Victor Lemoine in Nancy who, with his son Emile, went on to become one of the most widely renowned peony breeders in the world. 'Sarah Bernhardt' (1906), 'Le Cygne' (1907) and 'Primevere' (1907) are only three of those he produced whose names are legendary. One of the few breeders to work at making interspecific crosses, he did achieve a cross between *Paeonia lactiflora* (called *P. albiflora* at the time) and *P. wittmanniana* to produce successful hybrids, two of which are 'Le Printemps' (1905), a single with creamy-yellow blooms that make good cut flowers, and 'Avant Garde' (1907), a single with mauve-pink flowers and dark red stems.

In addition, the Lemoines succeeded in making a cross between *Paeonia lutea*, a tree peony with yellow flowers brought from China in the 1880s, and a *Paeonia suffruticosa* variety (also a tree peony). This resulted in the creation of a new class of peony known as *P. x lemoinei*, which was revolutionary because it introduced yellow into the color spectrum of new hybrid tree peonies. This first cross was the precursor to a series of lovely plants with delicate shadings of apricot, primrose, yellow and blush.

The herbaceous peonies 'Laura Dessert' (fragrant creamy double), introduced in 1913, and 'Auguste Dessert' (fragrant semi-double pink, 1920), come from another French dynasty of peony specialists. Etienne Mechin had been collecting peonies since 1840. Later his grandson, Auguste Dessert, joined him in the

BELOW: Paeonia mlokosewitschii.

family nursery at Chenonceaux and continued his grandfather's work, bringing his own flair to the production of new varieties.

Interestingly, though, until the 20th century by far the largest number of peony varieties in existence in both the East and the West were the result of careful selection and propagation of plants that had occurred naturally as seedlings. Many of the successful varieties have had a long "shelf life," and the legacy of all these talented plantsmen is enjoyed by gardeners around the world today.

In this respect the peony is unlike other venerable plants, such as roses and carnations, which, much earlier, had had their genes deliberately engineered by humans to create hybrids between different species. It is only in the course of the last hundred years that peony breeders have succeeded in creating true hybrids, and as already described, not until 1948 was the legendary cross between a tree peony and a herbaceous variety achieved.

4 Breaking New Ground

The Development of Modern Hybrids

Peonies in North America

Ornamental herbaceous peonies first went to the United States in the late 1700s, precious roots traveling with pioneers and planted as a reminder of faraway homes in the Old World. Mention of them occurs in Thomas Jefferson's gardening notebooks.

As in Britain and Europe, in America an explosion of interest in peonies occurred part way through the 19th century. By the early 1900s, the United States had become the world's major peony producer. As interest grew in these fascinating flowers from the East, so too did the desire to produce always more varieties, though it seems few people attempted to make deliberate crosses between species. New varieties came from seedlings, usually *Paeonia lactiflora* types, that had been pollinated by bees, grown on and assessed for their garden worthiness and the appeal of their flowers.

As the 19th century drew to a close, increasing numbers of growers were raising seedlings on both sides of the Atlantic. Initially, only the best were selected, named, propagated and advertised, but as demand grew and the United States became predominant, more growers became involved. Seedlings flooded on to the

OPPOSITE: An enviable outdoor arrangement at Keukenhof.

RIGHT: 'Miss America' teams up with a mauve bearded iris.

market, many of them produced by American growers, and many others imported from Europe. Quality varied enormously, and the naming of cultivars had become very confused.

In 1902 there was a move by concerned peony growers to try to establish some kind of standard by which peonies could be judged according to their quality and marketed appropriately. This move resulted in the formation of the American Peony Society in the following year, and its officers immediately set about compiling peony records, including those produced by European growers as well as Americans. Auguste Dessert, from France, made up a list of more than 500 authentic French and Belgian varieties of peonies. To this were added another 300 varieties from Kelway in Britain as well as many introduced by well-known U.S. breeders.

The next step was to cooperate with the Horticultural Society of Cornell University in the establishment of an experimental garden where all the authentic varieties could be studied over a period of years. Almost two thousand were received in the first year, and the task began of sorting out correct naming. This work took several years but proved to be a valuable exercise. Almost all the widely grown cultivars of the time appeared under more than one name. Examples of 'Edulis Superba' alone arrived at the test garden under 23 different names.

Over the years, many prominent peony growers have served as officers of the American Peony Society, and the numerous new peonies they introduced serve as reminders of their efforts. The society was not very old before three of its members independently experimented with crosses between *Paeonia lactiflora*, the Chinese peony, and the old species *P. officinalis*. They all went on to introduce important new cultivars, some of them a result of this cross.

Edward Auten was initially a banker and businessman, but early in life he started a peony nursery. Over a period of 40 years he named and introduced about 250 Chinese varieties as well as about 50 hybrids. Auten was best known for his unfading reds, and 'Chocolate Soldier' (*Paeonia lactiflora* x *P. officinalis*), a dark red with golden centers, usually Japanese in form, lives on as one of the reminders of his work.

Lyman Glasscock of Illinois likewise introduced peonies whose popularity has lasted through the decades. What started as a hobby became a business, and he was involved in growing and hybridizing peonies over a long period, although he began his working life as a bricklayer. His most famous variety is probably 'Red Charm', a double red *Paeonia lactiflora* x *P. officinalis* that has won the coveted American Peony Society gold medal. With another interesting cross between *Paeonia officinalis* 'Otto Froebel' and *P. tenuifolia*, Glasscock produced 'Laddie', which has a single, bright red flower and the finely dissected foliage and short stature (12 in./30 cm) of its species parent.

Of the three pioneers in this field, however, Professor Arthur Saunders is the

BELOW: A perennial favorite, 'Red Charm' is classified as a bomb type.

best known and made the greatest contribution to 20th-century hybridizing of peonies. Born in Canada in 1869, he received his doctorate in chemistry at Johns Hopkins University in Baltimore and in 1900 was appointed professor of chemistry at Hamilton College, in Clinton, New York, a post that he retained until his retirement in 1939. He joined the American Peony Society in 1906 and served as a director, almost without a pause, until his death in 1953.

In the early years of the century Professor Saunders worked with Chinese peonies, raising seedlings as many other breeders had done. By about 1915 he had managed to import several peony species from Europe—*Paeonia lutea*, the wild tree peony, arrived in 1913 from Lemoine in France; *Paeonia officinalis lobata* (see later), *P. macrophylla* and *P. mlokosewitschii* arrived soon afterward. Plant collectors and botanical gardens in Europe continued to send him wild peonies from the borders of the Mediterranean, the Caucasus, the Himalayas and China, many of which had never before been seen in the United States. Professor Saunders set to work to effect crosses with all the species he could acquire, though a full 80 percent of his hybrids had *Paeonia lactiflora* as one parent.

Most of Saunders's deliberate hybrids were done between the years 1917 and 1937, when he was 48 to 68 years old and still actively teaching chemistry. His aim was to "produce early flowering types in greater variety and beauty than we have heretofore had."

It was perhaps in the variety of new colors that arose from Saunders's hybrids that the most spectacular advances were made. No longer were peonies merely red: vermilion, scarlet and cerise entered the range. An entirely new spectrum of pinks appeared in the herbaceous hybrids—shades of salmon, coral, flamingo and

BELOW LEFT: The seedpods of peonies are attractive in their own right and who knows what treasures they hold within?

BELOW: Gorgeous golden bloom of *Paeonia lutea* var. *ludlowii* (syn. *P. delavayi ludlowii*).

cherry—which had formerly only existed in tree peony varieties. Many of these arresting colors resulted from crosses he made using *P. officinalis lobata*, a plant that had come to him from England in 1928, with *P. lactiflora*. The so-called lobata hybrids were among his most successful.

Saunders eventually developed more than 17,000 cultivars, including over 300 named varieties. Tree peonies too were part of his hybridization program, and he introduced more than 70 of these hybrids as well.

The United States also had its share of peony "dynasties." Oliver Brand opened a nursery in Minnesota in 1867 and started growing peonies. He and his son Archie produced some distinguished American varieties, including 'Longfellow' (1907), a late-blooming double red that makes a good cut flower, and 'David Harum' (1907), also a double red, flowering in mid-season.

The Wild nursery in Missouri was started at about that time, and three more generations of the family continued in the business until 1991. Altogether they introduced 40 new forms.

With even earlier beginnings is the Klehm dynasty, whose nursery business was started in Chicago in 1852 by German immigrant John Klehm and continues today under the name of Song Sparrow Farm and Nursery. Present owner Roy Klehm, whose son Kit now works with him, has continued the family tradition of breeding peonies. With William Krekler, he has produced, among others, some unusual flowers with twisted petals like 'Cherry Luau' and 'Twitterpated'. The latter flower is a soft pink with cherry and raspberry-red streaking on twisted, fringed petals. Some would say it has the appearance of a wildflower.

On the west coast, Allan Rogers and his family in Portland, Oregon, were already established in the peony business when Saunders's collection was broken up. They bought a significant number of his plants and continued working with

BELOW RIGHT: Forever favorite red and white.

BELOW: 'Red Grace', before it has fully opened out to a bomb.

OPPOSITE: A sensational field of 'Coral Sunset', a peony that thrives in New Zealand.

ABOVE: 'Coral Charm' glows with warmth.

them. Some of the *P. suffruticosa* tree peonies they bought were more than 50 years old, with roots as long as 4 ft. (1.2 m) when they were transferred with the help of a front-end loader.

These peony producers contributed to making the United States the peony hybridization capital of the world during the second half of the 20th century.

Popular colors with American growers

As with any genus in the plant world, the popularity of different colors waxes and wanes. In the 1950s and 1960s white was popular. 'Bowl of Cream' and 'Bridal Gown', bred by Carl Klehm, and 'Princess Bride', 'Fringed Ivory' and 'Moon over Barrington', bred by his son Roy, were the height of fashion.

More recently coral has been the sought-after shade, especially in the cut-flower range of peonies, with varieties such as 'Etched Salmon' (Cousins/Klehm, 1981), a big double flower; 'Pink Hawaiian Coral' (Klehm, 1984), a fragrant variety with flowers fading to a soft pink; 'Coral Charm' (Wissing, 1964); and 'Coral Sunset' (Wissing and Carl Klehm, 1981), considered by Roy Klehm to be the best coral.

Often the colors we can't have are the ones we want the most. Yellow peony cultivars have existed for more than a hundred years, since the tree peony *P. lutea* was discovered and used to inject yellow coloring into tree peony crosses. More recently, developments have seen a variety of yellow herbaceous peonies being introduced. The herbaceous species *P. wittmanniana* can lay claim to a slight yellow coloration, as can *P. mlokosewitschii* and *P. macrophylla*, and although these species have been used in the past by breeders, notably Professor Arthur Saunders, to introduce yellow into hybrids, they are still relatively rare.

The following are a few yellow hybrids that are at present available (although expensive) in North America.

See Appendix 1 at the end of the book for a list of yellow cultivars.

'Claire de Lune'. This is a cross between old French double pink peony 'M. Jules Elie' and the yellow species peony *P. mlokosewitschii*. The result is a pale yellow, single peony of about average height that flowers early in the season. Blooms are cupped and the petals slightly crinkled. 'Claire de Lune' was bred in 1954 by Dr. E.B. White, who apparently was very persistent in his attempts to cross *P. lactiflora* with *P. mlokosewitschii*—reputedly a very difficult and frustrating exercise.

'Daystar'. This is a single, pale yellow peony resulting from the work of Professor Saunders. Though the foliage gives few clues to its parentage, this peony is the result of a cross made between *P. tenuifolia* (often called the fern-leaf peony) and *P. mlokosewitschii*. The plant is of average height and blooms early in the peony season.

'**Early Glow**'. This new introduction (1992) from Don Hollingsworth resulted from a cross made between 'Roselette's Grandchild' and 'Cream Delight'. Again, *P. mlokosewitschii* features in the background of both parents. It is a single, slightly cupped bloom, with a somewhat fragile appearance, that appears early in the peony season.

'**Goldilocks**'. A cross between 'Haung Jin Lun' and 'Claire de Lune', this flower is fully double and light yellow. The plant was registered with the American Peony Society in 1975 by Ben Gilbertson. This peony has a double dose of yellow pigment—both parents are considered yellow. The breeder described it as having no fragrance, and being similar to 'Oriental Gold' above ground but without the distinctive yellow shading of its roots.

'**Haung Jin Lun**'. Known variously (and sometimes erroneously) as 'Aurea', 'Goldmine', 'Golden Wheel', 'Minuet', 'Oriental Gold' and 'Yokihi'—this is a double-flowered peony, looking somewhat like an old-fashioned rose, whose flowers are definitely light yellow. The roots also are a distinctive shade of yellow. It is assumed to be an old Chinese cultivar.

'**Lemon Chiffon**'. Like 'Goldilocks', this peony produces fully double pale yellow flowers. It was the grand champion at the American Peony Society's 2000 show. It seems to have *P. mlokosewitschii* in its background, though at least two generations back, and originated from Reath's Nursery in Michigan in 1981.

'**Nova**' and '**Nova II**'. These peonies were introduced by the U.S. breeder Professor A.P. Saunders in 1950 as a strain (i.e., a group of several similar peonies with similar breeding) resulting from second-generation crosses of *P. mlokosewitschii* x *P. macrophylla*. The flowers are small, single, cup-shaped and pale but distinct yellow. The plants are of below-average height and very early bloomers.

'**Prairie Moon**'. This is a hard-to-find, semi-double, palest yellow peony. The flower form is variable as flowers may range from single to semi-double on the same plant. It has no noticeable fragrance and the foliage is bright green, displaying to perfection the pale yellow hue of the flowers. Ancestors of 'Prairie Moon' (Fay, 1959) include *Paeonia lactiflora*, *P. macrophylla* and *P. peregrina*.

'**Summer Glow**'. This flower is scarcely yellow, but in the words of its breeder, Don Hollingsworth, it "opens peachy light yellow, passing to yellow white as the flower ages out of doors." Its ancestry includes *P. lactiflora* and *P. mlokosewitschii*. 'Summer Glow' was registered in 1992.

BELOW: 'Bowl of Cream'.

Herbaceous Peonies in the Garden

5

Alice Harding, the U.S. doyenne of peony growers at the beginning of the 20th century, considered that "no garden can really be too small to hold a peony. Had I but four square feet of ground at my disposal, I would plant a peony in the center and proceed to worship." No doubt, many other peony aficionados feel the same, and let's face it, dealing with a garden this small would be easy. Plant the peony, add a few small bulbs for late-winter color, an iris or two, and the garden is done. But most of us have more space than this, and most gardeners are greedy too. Having once fallen in love with peonies, we always want more. The challenge is how to organize more, so that each plant looks its best in the garden but still manages simultaneously to complement its close neighbors.

Gardeners are notoriously shortsighted. Most of us focus on our favorite plant of the moment to the exclusion of all else. So many people hear the word peony and start to drool. They go out and buy several, provide each one with a wide stretch of border, plant two tiny lobelias to keep the peony company and cultivate the earth around it lovingly all year. It looks neat, yes, and spectacular for two weeks—but what happens to the spirit of the garden after that? For the rest of the season the lonely peonies languish, ignored, their purpose in life forgotten.

OPPOSITE: 'Burma Ruby' glows with warmth.

RIGHT: 'Burma Ruby' in a late spring garden.

Don't do it. Peonies, more than most plants, need to be integrated into an overall plan.

William Robinson, he who declared in the 19th century how English gardens should be made, had a real feeling for peonies. In his classic *The English Flower Garden*, first published in 1883, he enunciates his grandiose ideas for them. Plant peonies as broad groups in new plantations, he says, among shrubs and low trees. These are the single or other less "noble" kinds he is talking about. When it comes to the sumptuous doubles, he advises special attention. "Give them a border all to themselves," he writes. Yes, we'd love to, but most of us don't have this kind of space. Borders, for his clients, often meant a patch of earth 300 ft. (90 m) long and about 6 ft. (1.8 m) wide.

He also argues the case for special gardens set aside for favorite perennials—peonies, for example—where they will not be overwhelmed or diminished in effect by their neighbors. Yes, of course he's right. Of course such plantings would make a spectacular sight for a few weeks in spring. But dreams are free! How many of us today have the freedom to treat peonies with such panache? And think of the dismal winter aspect with not a shred of greenery in sight. Most gardeners have to take the pragmatic approach of blending a selection of plants to create areas of year-round interest. It's a matter of choosing bedfellows that complement each other in form, color and seasons of interest.

Long-term planting plans

Herbaceous peonies don't particularly like being shifted. These are not your common wheelbarrow subjects who are happy to pull up roots and move at the whim of their gardener. So plan for the long term when you plant your peonies—they may still be there for your grandchildren to enjoy 50 years down the road.

Obviously herbaceous varieties look their best in late spring to early summer. They impart a certain excitement in early spring as they push their way through the earth in a rush of ruby or bronze curled fronds, not unlike an unfurling fern, but the true glory is in their blooms. Peonies in their prime are destined for

BELOW LEFT: Iris tectorum 'Alba' is the dainty iris growing with heucheras at the foot of 'Coral Sunset'.

BELOW MIDDLE: 'Coral Sunset' gradually fades to tone with white arum lilies.

BELOW RIGHT: Red and white peonies make a bold show.

stardom. They need to be situated where they can attract maximum admiration while they're in bloom. (No point having those fantastic flowers hidden by a fast-growing euphorbia.)

A show-off position for your favorite peony(ies) having been found, what's the next step? Now it's time to forget the blooms and consider foliage. This also is a feature of the plant and is around much longer than the flowers. Tough, textured and prolific, the leaves can make an attractive backdrop for the next round of flowering perennials. And later—in autumn—as the foliage turns to red, bronze or gold, the peony plant will call attention to itself again. Try to place the peony where its foliage will be highlighted. Give it a background such as a plastered wall, a dense, purple hedge of berberis perhaps, or clumps of conifers—though it is important that the shrubs or trees do not take all the moisture and nutrients away from the peonies.

Sizing considerations

The next decision relates to size of the neighboring plants. What other shrubs or perennials are appropriate to the dimensions of peonies? Remember, peonies keep expanding for several years, and as they mature the mass of blooms increases each season. Flowers usually extend beyond the foliage on strong stems.

Herbaceous peonies grow to between 2 and 4½ ft. (60 cm and 1.3 m) in height, becoming more bushy each season until they are about as wide as they are high. There are a few varieties that produce more than 30 stems when they are fully developed, but they need space to develop to this potential. Overcrowded peonies may eventually refuse to bloom. Ideally there needs to be about 4 ft. (1.2 m) between two peony plants, or between a peony and another shrub. This provides space for air to circulate and helps keep the dreaded botrytis at bay.

Among other plants, their natural place is in the middle section of a garden, with smaller things in front and taller ones behind. Note also that there are some peonies with weak stems and enormous flowers that tend to flop without extra support. If you choose these varieties, you need to consider some kind of support system that won't spoil the overall good looks of the plant. Commercial hoops are available, or you can devise your own system. Just remember that bits of string, old pantyhose, strangled plants and ugly stakes do not flatter any garden.

Good companions

Now, which other plants will enhance the peony bush and be enhanced by a close association? Think again about the foliage. Placing other plants with a similar outline and leaves of a similar size beside a peony will cause the whole to recede in a mish-mash of anonymity. I would never plant hellebores beside peonies, for example, because their foliage has a certain similarity.

Look for plants whose foliage and form will provide contrasts beside the

TOP: Gorgeous white 'Lancaster Imp' is a sought-after variety. 'Old Faithful' is popular as a cut flower in the Northern Hemisphere. New Zealand growers export it to the US for Christmas use.

MIDDLE: 'Flame', single and herbaceous, is an excellent choice planted in front of a dark hedge.

BOTTOM: Late spring and the peonies are in full flower.

peony. Plants with sword-shaped leaves are one group—phormiums, sisyrinchiums or irises, for example. Plants that can be trimmed easily to create solid shapes are another. A low hedge in front of peonies adds a note of formality and provides structure that remains when the peonies have gone to bed for the winter. The small leaves of buxus, escallonia and lonicera, or hebes such as *Hebe topiaria* or *H. buxifolia*, have just the right foliage to make a contrast with the broader, dissected leaves of peonies. Imagine the effect of the crimson blooms of 'Red Charm' or the cheerfulness of 'Coral Charm' appearing above the trimmed shape of such a green hedge.

Plants with tall, spire-shaped flowers also add variety of form among peonies, while climbers can go at their back and spring-flowering bulbs in front to provide color before the peonies bloom. Later the bushes will obscure the aging bulb foliage—but make sure that the bulb flowers are not so close to the peonies that late bloomers will be obscured. The developing peony seedpods add further interest, as does the autumn foliage. Remember, you want to be able to see these changes.

Once the peonies are in hibernation, there need to be other plants in the same area to provide a focus while they are sleeping. Even one deciduous tree with a fascinating silhouette can be that center of focus. Evergreen shrubs add density and, if well chosen, some interesting shapes.

Think too about how much sun and how much shade the peonies will get in relation to the other plants around them, particularly when overhanging trees form part of the picture. Peonies need freely circulating air to help prevent botrytis in humid weather, as well as at least half a day's sunshine.

If you're one of those lucky people who have space for a variety of peonies, you can stretch the weeks when you have them blooming in your garden by choosing cultivars that flower at different times. In a normal year, the total peony-flowering season extends from approximately mid-May until early July in the Northern Hemisphere (or October until December in the Southern), with one or two species flowering earlier in both hemispheres, and with tree peonies everywhere flowering earlier than their herbaceous siblings. Modern hybrids developed from the European species *Paeonia officinalis* and *P. mascula* have inherited the early-flowering characteristics of their progenitors; those derived from *P. lactiflora*, the Chinese species, generally flower later in the season. Plants that receive some shade during the day will also bloom later than those in full sunshine, and their blooms will retain their color better. A list of early- and later-flowering varieties appears in Appendix 1 on page 130.

Garden designers usually recommend planting perennials in family groups for greater effect, but after several years a herbaceous peony effectively forms its own "group," so single bushes can be planted throughout a shrubbery or perennial border without looking sparse. Each one will make an eye-catch-

BELOW: Late 'Windflower'.

BOTTOM: 'Garden Peace' fits easily into any color scheme or any style of garden.

ing display in flower, and the opportunity to color-coordinate them with their companions is part of the fun of working out your own design. If you have the space to plant peonies in groups, then so much the better.

Color has much to do with the feeling of a garden. White creates a cool look or a suggestion of the ethereal, especially at dusk. Crimson is a rich, formal color; scarlet is warm, cheerful, even fiery; coral suggests a more modern, sophisticated feeling; and pink, white and red mixed together impart a timeless, gentle, romantic atmosphere.

Large double blooms imply extravagance; small single blooms speak of simplicity or intimacy; large single blooms, a sense of sophistication. Choosing peonies with colors and form that will complement the ambience of the garden they are to live in will contribute to an integrated look.

Peony blooms are not only drop-dead gorgeous—many of them are also perfumed. Remember to take advantage of this in your design and use perfumed varieties near the house, in a courtyard or near an outdoor entertaining area. Enclosed areas usually trap the perfume and emphasize its effect. A short list of perfumed varieties also appears in Appendix 1.

ABOVE LEFT: The eternal appeal of blue and white: tree peony 'Renkaku' and aquilegia.

ABOVE: Herbaceous peonies in a spring garden.

Landscaping with Herbaceous Peonies

Borders and edgings

Old books written about peonies invariably talk of long and broad borders solid with peonies, some even providing specific planting plans, including bulbs for late winter interest. It's easy to imagine Edwardian ladies strolling along such a border, parasols in hand, long skirts elegantly trailing. Today, I imagine few such borders exist, and then only in spacious country gardens. But in a 21st-century version of this horticultural classic, one of our neighbors has a pathway, lined with peonies, leading to the front door. Cleverly, it includes other plants for year-round interest.

Nearest to the path is a low edging of *Buxus*. Next to it, and slightly taller, is a parallel planting of *Teucrium fruticans*, which has attractive, small silvery leaves and adapts easily to frequent clipping. Behind this is a row of the peony 'Hermione', taller again, which produces opulent double blooms that open pale shell pink. Backing these are white hydrangeas that start into flower once the peonies are over. Olive trees are planted at intervals among the peonies and are in tone with the walls of the house, which are a soft gray. The parallel rows of *Buxus* and *Teucrium* add texture, a gradation of color and, of course, structure as well as winter interest. The peonies add the froth and glamour. The effect is cool, elegant and sophisticated.

OPPOSITE: Peonies are showy plants for public gardens.

RIGHT: Roses combine with peonies to make a spectacular driveway border.

ABOVE: For those who like to hedge their peonies in, *Buxus* is a good choice.

This theme adapts easily to a variety of situations—a path curving alongside a driveway, the border to a lawn, or a double edging down both sides of a flight of steps.

Consider the effect of a continuous border of one of the coral peony varieties, perhaps with a ginkgo as the punctuation point at the end of the planting. A similar border could be created using the favorite old peony 'Rubra Plena', which has extravagant crimson double blooms and would look good finished off with a symmetrical conifer. For the romantics, a border in pink, white and red peonies might be terminated with a flowering cherry tree. A low hedge of bright green *Buxus* makes the perfect accompaniment to any of these combinations, and the result is a textured border planting, beside a boundary fence or along a driveway, that has seasonal high points.

Companion plants

When you're considering companion plants, think first about the shape of a peony bush. In general terms it has a rounded form; the flowers also are round and usually full. Choosing plants with contrasting shapes to bed down with the peonies creates impact and gives each plant an identity of its own. Choosing flowering times to span the season provides continuity.

When you see paintings of old cottage gardens, peonies are usually in the picture. Cottage gardens may be out of favor at present, but the plant combinations still work well. Look carefully and you'll see tall plants at the back—aquilegias, lupins and delphiniums. Their varied forms—tall, slender and dainty (in the case of aquilegias)—act as a counterpoint to the heavier peony. Bearded irises are often there too, and once their flowers have faded, the form of their bladelike leaves creates an interesting contrast with the peony foliage. All these plants bloom at a similar time. In front are shorter, more finely textured plants—dianthus, violas, maybe cranesbill geraniums, marigolds, forget-me-nots and cornflowers—that continue to flower through summer.

Flowering later than the peonies are roses, although some of the early *Rugosa* types may coincide with the flowering season of peonies. Roses also like to be treated as stars and enjoy similar conditions to peonies. Happily, their season continues on from the peonies, which means that they don't compete with their more flamboyant companions. (It has always puzzled me that people talk about "peony roses." Perhaps it's because some of the big double peonies resemble the extravagant cabbage roses of old.)

Lilies, including *Lilium candidum*, the gorgeous regal lilies and *Lilium longiflorum*, are also frequently seen as companions to peonies. Their slender height complements the bulk of a peony bush. Of course, lilies need to be planted behind the peonies. And remember to plant them in groups, or they will spend years looking lonely and lanky.

BELOW LEFT: Tall bearded irises and peonies usually flower at a similar time.

BELOW MIDDLE: Small-flowered geraniums make an interesting foil for big, bold, peony blooms.

BELOW: Carex testacea adds an element of the wild garden beside 'Raspberry Sundae'.

TOP: Using the same color but contrasting shapes is always a successful design element.

ABOVE RIGHT: Peonies and clematis: a match made in heaven.

ABOVE: By choosing varieties carefully, it is possible to have roses and peonies flowering at the same time.

For a more restrained look, make a planting of, say, three peony bushes set beside a clump of lupins in a toning color range—'Nymphe', for example, with its softly pink, single blooms set off by a white lupin variety; or the rich crimson, double *Paeonia officinalis* 'Rubra Plena' beside a pale blue lupin. Fill in around them with shrubs that flower at a different time—viburnums, lilac and *Choisya* for spring blooms; a dark-leafed holly for year-round foliage interest; English lavenders for summer froth and perfume. The leaves of 'Rubra Plena'—big, rich green and deeply cut—make it an attractive shrub for the whole season.

Peonies, combined with one or two other plants with interesting but less flamboyant flowers, are the perfect plant for a walled formal garden, where all the attention is on its contents and there is no distraction from a landscape beyond the borders. Simplicity is the note to aim for in this situation. Visualize symmetrical beds, trimmed with *Buxus* and bordered by paths. In each bed a different variety of peony is planted, staging the bloom time from early to late season. Color-coordinated with the peonies are Siberian irises, one of the most elegant and stately plants that exist, and climbing on the walls is clematis. The early-blooming 'Krinkled White', a glorious and somewhat fragile-looking flower; 'Sarah Bernhardt', double, pink, ruffled and very late blooming; 'Gay Paree', a late-flowering Japanese bloom in bright pink and pale cream—these are only three of any number of peonies that would work well in this type of situation.

Anne Scott-James, in her book *The Best Plants for Your Garden,* talks about clematis and peonies in her own patch. There the early-blooming species *Paeonia mlokosewitschii*, with single flowers of a clear lemon, is planted in a bed under an apple tree with blue *Clematis macropetala* climbing into its branches. The two come out at the same time.

Peonies are such spectacular plants that gardeners often have indelible memories of combinations in which they are the star attraction. Russell Page, English garden designer to the rich and famous 50 years ago, writes about a garden he saw in his youth at Hidcote, in England. "I remember a double border of old-fashioned roses combined with the equally old-fashioned *Paeonia officinalis*. The path between was edged with purple-mauve *Campanula portenschlagiana* and the mustard-green alchemilla which used to be called 'Lady's Mantle'. In this unexpected combination these old-fashioned plants seemed to complement each other exactly and one sensed the result of careful thought and a good understanding of the nature of the plants involved."

Plants themselves don't change over time. It is the way we group them that changes and adds a particular imprint. The grouping that Page mentions would look appealing today, and the combination of purple and sharp green is right in line with the present emphasis on bright colors.

Gardeners seeking a modern, minimalist look could try combining peonies with the narrow, sword-shaped foliage of phormiums (flax). I saw a garden once in which the peony 'Burma Ruby' mingled with a hybrid, red-leafed New Zealand flax and a heuchera with garnet-colored foliage. The effect was memorable.

BELOW LEFT: Coral companions; color coordinated peonies and azaleas.

BELOW: Peonies always fit in a formal garden.

A themed garden

White flowers have an eternal appeal, and white peonies are no exception. The gorgeous *Paeonia lactifolia* 'Duchesse de Nemours' was introduced as long ago as 1856, but it is still one of the most popular peonies today. With luscious big double blooms and the added bonus of perfume, it makes a good garden subject as well as an excellent cut flower. 'Kelway's Glorious', another double white, is similarly flamboyant.

At the other end of the scale between opulence and modesty is the single-flowered species *Paeonia emodi*, which in its utter simplicity is just as stunning as the Duchess, as is the single 'Early Windflower', a hybrid from *P. emodi*. Slightly more exotic, but still single, is 'Krinkled White'. These three singles all flower early in the season; the double-flowered varieties later. In groups, these five plants provide variety, perfume and an extended flowering time. To add a more exotic touch—and an even earlier bloom—include the white-flowered tree peony 'Renkaku'. With flowers like this to play with, peonies make excellent subjects for a white and silver garden.

Using the peonies as a base, the designer could add many other plants to the scheme for a white garden. White bearded irises with peonies are stunning. The flowers complement each other with their contrasting form, and the iris foliage endures through summer. Add *Anthemis punctata* ssp. *cupaniana* at their feet. This perennial has daisy-like flowers and attractive silver-gray dissected foliage that acts as a good weed deterrent. For fill-in plants there are any number of silver-gray–foliaged varieties. Examples include artemisias, especially the lacy *Artemisia alba* 'Canescens' and the bolder-leafed *A. ludoviciana* 'Valerie Finnis' (which can be invasive); dianthus ('Alan Titchmarsh' has white flowers, as does 'White Lady', 'Haytor White' or the old-fashioned 'Charles Musgrave'); and lamb's ear (*Stachys byzantina*), with its velvety gray leaves.

Oriental lilies would be suitable for planting behind the peonies. They bloom in late summer, and most varieties have a delicious perfume. 'Casablanca', with flaring trumpets textured like heavy silk and a heavenly fragrance, has a sensuality that makes a perfect follow-on from the equally sensual peonies. Behind

BELOW RIGHT:
'Lonesome Dove' and 'Gay Paree'.

BELOW: Herbaceous peony 'Dutch Dwarf' is a low-growing hybrid (to about 2 ft. or 60 cm).

the lilies you could plant the deciduous weeping silver pear *Pyrus salicifolia* 'Pendula' (zones 5–9), an elegant tree that suits small gardens.

In a Mediterranean climate (zones 8 and 9), as background and with foliage that endures through winter, plant olive trees to add an element of grace. In a colder climate you might choose the silvery-blue *Picea pungens* (zones 3–8) in one of its smaller forms.

Peonies in pots

In theory, almost any plant can be grown successfully in a container (I grow *Pinus radiata* in tubs, and they are most often considered a forest tree), so growing a peony in a big pot, be it a herbaceous variety or a tree peony, should present no problems. There are, however, some definite prerequisites. Most importantly, the gardener has to be committed to keeping the plant healthy—no container plants thrive on neglect. It is also very important to choose a container large enough to provide plenty of space for the peony to develop its root structure. Anything smaller than a half wine barrel is probably too small. Excellent drainage is non-negotiable and, as with any container-grown plant, it must have regular and adequate moisture and sustenance.

TOP LEFT: Dainty crimson astrantias complement a late-flowering bloom.

TOP & MIDDLE: A single white herbaceous peony makes an excellent companion beside the frillier blooms of a white bearded iris and the daisy flowers of *Anthemis cupaniana*.

BOTTOM: 'Lonesome Dove'.

Garden soil on its own is not suitable in pots because it tends to compact quickly and prevent the water from penetrating evenly, but as a medium it can be mixed with equal amounts of aged leaf mold or well-matured compost and fine gravel or sand. It should also contain slow-release fertilizer capsules—this is the easiest way to ensure that pot-grown plants receive food over an extended period. In subsequent years these can be scattered over the surface of the container and gently worked into the mix. Some gardeners also like to add water-retention products to the mix. I'm not convinced that these are greatly effective. A good commercial potting mix that contains plenty of fine gravel or ground pumice/perlite to keep it friable is also suitable.

Liquid feeding (or "fertigating") is another effective way of maintaining container-grown plants, but success relies on the constancy of the gardener. If you choose this method then you should feed the plant about every three weeks during the growing season.

When watering container plants it's not enough to wait until the water seeps out of the bottom. Often the water finds its own thin route to the bottom of the tub, and the mix around the resulting rivulet is quite dry. You really need to scratch beneath the surface and check that the mix is evenly damp to a reasonable depth before you are satisfied the plant has received enough water.

It's taken me many years of container growing to learn not to fill the tub, pot, barrel or whatever right to the top with potting mix. By leaving at least 3 in. (7.5 cm) from the top of the container to the surface of the soil, it's possible to flood it and let the water seep down gradually. Repeating this maneuver several times at one watering usually allows for good penetration.

A layer of coarsely broken pottery shards or large-size gravel in the bottom of the container is a good way to assist reliable drainage. This layer can be topped with another of slightly finer gravel before the potting mix is added.

Just as it is best to plant peonies in the garden in the fall, so fall is the best time to plant them in pots. At this stage of the year, they make the bulk of their new root growth.

Where freezing temperatures (below zone 7) occur over winter, peonies in containers will most likely not survive without being moved to a protected place. They need to experience enough chill to cause dormancy, but deep-freeze conditions will kill the root system.

Because the tubs will be displayed in a prominent position, it is best to choose peony varieties that bloom for as long as possible. These are the varieties that have more than one bud per stem and therefore produce more flowers over a longer period. 'Kelway's Glorious', 'Jeanne d'Arc' and 'Baroness Schroeder' are all free-flowering and fragrant, as well as neat, compact plants, making them ideal varieties to grow in tubs, especially on a patio or in a courtyard or walled garden, close to a barbecue area or near the house, where their fragrance and flowers can be enjoyed.

Container companions

To provide some color when the peonies are hibernating, bulbs can be planted in the tubs around the edge. Snowdrop lovers and crocus enthusiasts can choose a selection of their favorite varieties to create miniature glory when the peony is still well asleep. There are also various tiny irises that flower at the end of winter—*Iris danfordiae* is one; *I. reticulata* and its cultivars are others.

To add interest and color just as the peony foliage is getting ready to unfold, plant dwarf daffodils, particularly the *Narcissus cyclamineus* varieties and *N. bulbocodium*, the hoop-petticoat daffodil, or dwarf tulips such as *Tulipa tarda* with yellow petals tipped with white. Small-leafed primulas make an attractive follow-on from the bulbs and later in the season enjoy the shade cast by the peony foliage.

Violas are an easy-care option as tub edgings. There is a wide range of varieties, all of which put out their first blooms in early spring and carry on right over summer if they have sufficient moisture. 'Maggie Mott', with blooms of mid-mauve, is a dependable favorite; 'Jackanapes' is cheerful in purple and gold; and the perennial white-flowered viola has a classic appeal.

Trailing plants are another option. Arabis, either the single or double-flowered variety, is in bloom at the same time as tree peonies. Forget-me-nots and corydalis, with their dainty blue flowers, also bloom at the same time as the early peony varieties and make attractive footnotes to the larger flowers. The alpine strawberry does well in containers; it has attractive foliage and the added appeal of small, bright, sweet fruit that appears about the time the peony blooms are over for the season. Trailing petunias give a long season of summer color and can be persuaded to climb, mingling with the peony foliage.

For those who don't like understory planting, mulching the tub with small rocks or bark chips will help to conserve moisture, but small plants used as ground cover in a tub have the advantage of acting as an early-warning system for moisture control. If the ground cover is wilting, it's a sure sign that the peony will need water too.

BELOW LEFT: The foliage of *Paeonia lithophila* is finely cut and fernlike. Its size makes it an ideal container plant.

BELOW: Delicate foliage of *Paeonia lithophila* with erythroniums.

7 Herbaceous Peonies— Care and Cosseting

"Why grow peonies?" ask some gardeners. "Their flowering season is so short and they die down in winter." Yes, but they bring glory in their wake. And we all need doses of glory—by definition, a transient state. As well as their magnificent and often fragrant flowers, most have attractive foliage, often tinted bronze when new and taking on reddish or purple tones as autumn advances. They're interesting plants for a large part of the year. They are also long-lived, though sometimes slow-growing at first.

Climate

Peonies' large showy flowers, in many colors and forms, are produced in mid- to late spring. They need winter chilling to induce a period of dormancy, and most herbaceous peonies will do well in zones 3–8. However, in cold zones mulching on top of the roots helps to protect the peony—not so much from cold as from quick changes in temperature, which are likely to occur. In zones 3–5, herbaceous peonies should be planted more deeply than in warmer areas. Place the tallest eye tip about 2 in. (5 cm) below the surface.

Too much heat is generally more of a problem than too much cold, so it is

OPPOSITE: **The perfect garden party arrangement at Keukenhof.**
RIGHT: **'Highlights'.**

ABOVE LEFT: Peony fields in New Zealand in late November.

ABOVE MIDDLE: 'Gay Paree' grows with 'Lois Kelsey', an unusual white peony with 'shredded' petals.

ABOVE RIGHT: Peony buds, full of promise, make punctuation marks in a spring garden.

essential to choose peony varieties most suited to your climate. This is especially important for gardeners in zone 9 who are desperate to try growing peonies. Early-blooming varieties that flower before the temperatures rise too high, and single or Japanese cultivars, generally perform better in warmer areas. Afternoon shade will protect flowers from fading too quickly in hot areas. Big double blooms, however, need hot sun to bring them out fully; not enough and they may rot. Singles and Japanese flower forms survive better in rainy climates, where plants producing big, heavy, double flowers that fill with rain and droop are not a good choice.

In the southern United States, where there is heavy rainfall and the temperature often reaches above 90°F (32°C) during the summer, peonies should be able to grow and bloom in spring, but they need some help. Excellent drainage, sufficient ventilation and semi-shade are all necessary. Planting them on the north side of a building is one way to give them a cooler environment.

In cold climates the stems of herbaceous peonies are killed by frost if they have not been cut to the ground before the onset of winter. In warmer climates—zone 9 where there is no frost—the gardener may need to simulate dormancy by cutting herbaceous stems off near the ground in autumn, in time for the peony root to gain about three months of dormancy. Some growers go to the lengths of lifting the flowers' roots and storing them in a refrigerator over winter. This takes true commitment—and a special-purpose refrigerator.

Some newer varieties that should flower in warmer areas include 'Abalone Pearl', 'Coral Charm', 'Do Tell' and 'Miss America'. For more examples, see Appendix 1 on page 130.

How to choose peonies

Once you have decided what type of peony suits your climate, there all sorts of other decisions to be made. If you have space for several plants then you will probably want to enjoy their blooms for as long as possible, so a selection from early- to late-blooming varieties is a good idea.

The next decision relates to color. Do you want light, bright or pastel? Dark, dramatic or dynamic? Then there are different forms to consider: bowl-shaped, single, double, Japanese, or some of everything.

Plants that perform well are probably a prerequisite, and any that have been awarded the American Peony Society Gold Medal will fulfill this requirement. Fragrance is also an important criterion for many gardeners.

If you are ordering bare roots by mail order, confirm that they will arrive in plenty of time for you to plant them before harsh weather sets in.

Soil and siting

Peonies generally like a sunny situation in well-fertilized soil and, although they are not too fussy, a pH of between 6 and 7 is ideal. In general, excellent drainage is essential, though the *Lactiflora* hybrids will tolerate heavier soil and a little more moisture than some of the European varieties, especially in summer. In areas where snow lies on the ground in winter, beware of soggy soil caused by thaws.

Either sandy soil or clay that is not too compacted is suitable, but heavy soil needs to be broken up—not just where the roots are planted initially, but over a wide enough area to allow them to spread easily as they mature. Some plants that thrive for the first few years and then falter may have a problem with maintaining root development in impenetrable soil. The addition of well-rotted compost, old manure, bone meal, seaweed, leaf mold or other organic materials improves the soil and, if deeply dug in, helps the plant to form a strong root system—very important in areas where winters are harsh. Some growers claim that flower color is better on plants grown in clay soils, but the addition of humus-rich material is still necessary.

Like roses, peonies should not be replanted where another variety grew previously. If you remove a peony and replace it with another in the same spot, the old soil should be dug out and new soil provided.

Most varieties like at least half a day's sun, though some, including anemone-flowered peonies, which like rich loam, thrive under deciduous fruit trees, for example. However, the dense shade of overhanging trees such as oak or beech is not conducive to happy plants. Lack of sufficient air circulation is likely to encourage botrytis in damp or humid weather.

Peonies tend to be greedy plants and gobble up the goodies from the soil, but if planted too closely to other greedy plants—hedges, trees, big shrubs—these perennials may come off second best in the grab for sustenance. Planted in a border, the large flowering varieties need at least 3 ft. (1 m) between individual plants as they take several years to reach their adult size. On average, peonies grow about 3 ft. (1 m) tall and attain similar dimensions in width. Any gaps while they are growing can be filled with annuals or short-lived perennials that you can remove once the peonies need that space.

Tall varieties may need to be provided with grow-through support early in the season. For those with long stems and big, heavy flowers, semicircular

BELOW: **Peonies don't have to be blowsy or bombastic to make an impact.**

ABOVE RIGHT: 'Coral 'n Gold', early to mid-season.

ABOVE: 'Coral Charm' has enjoyed a long run of popularity as both a garden subject and a cut flower.

perennial supports with long legs made from coated metal can be inserted into the earth around the plant during spring and easily removed later.

Planting

Plan carefully before you plant your peony. They have been known to live happily in the same spot for more than 50 years, and they strongly resent having their roots disturbed.

How you plant your peonies depends on timing. New plants can be purchased either as potted specimens year-round or as bare roots in early fall, which is the preferred time to plant. This is when the peonies begin growing thin white feeder roots that help the plant get through winter. Planting them ahead of the cold weather gives time for these roots to get well established before the need arises to put out new stems. If you buy bare roots, it's a good idea to soak them overnight to replace lost moisture, though any that display shriveled roots are not a good buy.

If you buy plants in spring, each peony will be potted up, preferably in a good rich mix. The peony can either be left in its pot until fall (with appropriate care) or planted into the ground—root-ball, earth and all—so that the whole plant is disturbed as little as possible.

The most important thing to remember is not to plant your peony too deeply or it will sulk.

Most herbaceous peonies that fail to flower have been set in the ground too deeply. When planting crowns (or bare roots), dig a hole 12–18 in. (30–45 cm) deep and 12 in. (30 cm) wide. Replace part of the soil in a mound and spread the roots over it. Make sure they are not upside down, and set them so that the tip of the eyes (swollen pink or reddish buds) will be no more than 1 in. (2.5 cm) below the surface of the soil. Firm the soil in well around the roots, eliminating air pockets, and water thoroughly.

Some growers suggest that the tips should actually be visible above ground. Luckily the crown has a number of latent buds. If you accidentally knock off the primary buds during planting, new ones, dormant until now, will grow to replace them. In late summer new crown buds form and food is stored in the tuberous roots for the following season.

Divisions with three to five eyes will reach maturity sooner than smaller divisions. If one- or two-eye divisions are used, it may be several years before the plant flowers.

Water peonies thoroughly and regularly for the first year to encourage deep rooting. In time they will develop large storage roots that help them get through the hot summer months. Once they are well established, peonies are drought-resistant—though moisture in spring is important for producing good flowers. After bloom time, the peony requires less water. Be sure the area around the roots drains well.

One New Zealand grower who specializes in growing peony tubers for sale and whose peony farm is in a windy, dry area of the country, has not given her crop any supplementary irrigation since 1992, and the tubers do well.

Peonies like to be fed in spring, when the stems are about 2–3 in. (5–7.5 cm) high. Use either a low nitrogen, complete fertilizer such as 5–10–5 or 5–10–10 at the rate of 2–3 pounds per 100 sq. ft. (1–1.3 kg per 9 m²), or alternatively apply well-rotted manure on the soil surface around the plant. Never let fertilizer or fresh manure touch the stems as it may burn them. One grower reports success by sprinkling 2 tablespoons (30 mL) of sulfate of potash around young peony bushes, watering them well and mulching them with a layer of old manure, leaf mold or compost. The potash promotes good health and flower color; the mulch helps to keep the roots moist.

BELOW: New peony foliage adds interest to the spring garden and carries the promise of later beauty.

If mulch is placed over the roots in autumn, it should not be so thick that it prevents the circulation of air. A grower in zone 8 finds it works well to cover her dormant roots in winter with a mulch of well-rotted manure to act as winter protection; in early spring she draws it aside, where it will not impede the growth of new shoots but where the rain run-off can still feed them.

When you work around the plants in the early spring, be careful of the tender emerging shoots. They will usually be dark red.

All peonies are not born equal. Some will mature quickly, putting on maybe 10 stems in three years with roots extending up to 2 ft. (60 cm) beyond the center of the crown. Others may produce only four stems in the same period, with roots only 12 in. (30 cm) long. There is an old saying about peonies: first year sleep, second year creep, third year leap. Good peony growers are patient growers.

Bushes should start to flower by the third season after planting, and from then on the show just keeps on improving. Plants grown for garden display, where the aim is to have as many flowers as possible over as long a period as possible, do not need disbudding. Those who want gorgeous cut flowers to boast about should pinch off the lateral or side buds as they form, leaving only the terminal or top buds. Don't despair if your double peonies flower as singles in their first year—they just need to grow up. As with wine, the more mature the peony plant, the more enticing it becomes.

Dividing and moving peony plants

For some unexplained reason, the ancient Greeks believed it was dangerous practice to pull peony roots out of the ground. If it had to be done at all, then the roots were to be gathered at the dead of night, lest woodpeckers see the digger at work and peck out his eyes. (Why woodpeckers specifically, I'm not sure.) And what's more, these early gardeners believed that the groaning of a peony root as it was pulled out of the ground was a sound fatal to anyone who heard it. Be warned!

If you absolutely have to divide or move your peonies, do so in fall, around mid-September in the Northern Hemisphere (mid-March in the Southern Hemisphere), when the plants naturally begin putting on new roots prior to going dormant. Digging and dividing at this time of the year is less stressful for the peonies than during spring, when plants are putting on lots of new growth, or during the heat of summer. It allows each plant some time to adjust to a new home before winter chills set in.

Under the soil, the peony is a tangle of large and small fleshy, tapered storage roots as well as a host of small feeder roots, which are often not seen because they have disappeared or been separated from the clump in the process of excavating. Once dug up, the roots need to be carefully handled. Divisions, for some reason, do better than a whole plant that has been dug up and moved.

For details on dividing peonies, see Chapter 11, page 114.

End-of-season care

Although peony seedheads are attractive, it's a good idea to remove them after flowering to allow the plant to store more energy for next year's bloom, unless of course you want to save the seed.

At the end of fall, when the foliage has lost its color, cut it back and burn it (if permissible) or put it in the garbage can (not the compost bin) to avoid any fungus spores settling in the soil over winter. Also cut back the old stalks to

BELOW: 'Hermione' not yet fully open.

just below ground level to prevent disease spores from sitting in the base of the stalks all winter, waiting to attack in spring. The new season's growth buds are close to the base of the old stalks. Carefully scratching away the earth at the crown will uncover these buds so you can avoid damaging them in the process of cutting back.

Winter is the time to sit in front of a fire and dream about the glory that your peonies will present to you in spring.

Tree Peonies—
The "King of Flowers"

8

An English writer once called the tree peony, or moutan, the "king of all butter-cups." Botanically speaking, the writer was correct in his time, for peonies were once classified as part of the family of Ranunculaceae. But the botanists—as they are wont to do—have re-sorted the Ranunculaceae, and happily *Paeonia* has been dignified with a family all to itself. Thinking of any peony as a mere buttercup belittles the magnificent blooms they produce, and tree peonies were christened much more generously by the Chinese centuries ago as the "King of Flowers."

The tree peony also came to represent prosperity, so it is not surprising that the emperors of various Chinese dynasties surrounded themselves with moutans. The grounds of the imperial palaces were planted with peonies in the thousands. Even today, the Emperor's Palace in the Forbidden City in Beijing is alight every spring with a magnificent display of tree peonies in full bloom.

Cultivated for its spectacular beauty and for its traditional place in Chinese culture, the tree peony is farmed extensively in China today for is medicinal value. The fragile-looking beauty, 'Fen(g) Dan Bai' ('Phoenix White'), exported to North America as a garden plant, also fills fields in Szechuan with its glorious white fragrant flowers, although it is the roots that are farmed. Their bark is an ingredient of

*OPPOSITE: **Paeonia rockii** with a background of hawthorn.*

LEFT: **A seedling *Paeonia delavayi.***

TOP: 'Haku banryu', a well-known Japanese tree peony.

MIDDLE: 'Souvenir du Professor Maxime Cornu' is an old French hybrid tree peony.

ABOVE: The apricot-buff colored tree peony 'Autumn Sunset' creates an effective foil for purple clematis.

a herbal medicine that is used by the Chinese for its antispasmodic qualities, and for its effectiveness in treating arthritis and dysentery.

History

Chinese origins

The earliest record of the tree peony dates back to evidence found in a first-century Chinese tomb, excavated in 1972. It is a prescription, written on a strip of bamboo, that advocates using the skin of a tree peony root to counteract blood clotting.

A garden scene that dates from the fourth century includes tree peonies in the background. Little did the painter Gu Kaizhi, who lived from 345 until 406, dream that his artistic efforts would be used centuries later to identify and date plants of his time.

No records of the parentage of these early Chinese tree peonies seem to exist and, after centuries of natural selection and possibly hand pollination, the progenitors of the moutan are an enigma. A Chinese author in AD 536 did, however, write that the original habitat of the wild plant was in eastern Szechuan and in Shensi in western China. Finding plants in the wild has long since been almost impossible.

Known in China as the moutan or mudan, this much-varying plant was well established in gardens by the year 700. A Chinese named Gow Yang Sew has gone down in history because of his studbook, *Mow Tan Poo*, which he produced in the 700s and which details about 30 varieties. Michael Haworth-Booth, in his book *The Moutan or Tree Peony*, reports that during the Tang Dynasty (AD 618–906) tree peonies were very fashionable and good ones fetched high prices. It was claimed that the variety 'Pi Leang Kin' actually sold for 100 ounces of gold—a foreshadowing of the Dutch tulipomania of the 17th century.

Early European developments

The first peonies in European gardens were herbaceous species. It was not until 1789 that the first tree peony arrived in Europe, brought to England by a doctor in the British East India Company who had been commissioned by Sir Joseph Banks to bring one back from the East. It was subsequently planted at Kew Gardens, to be joined later by two other varieties in 1794 and 1797.

Charles Greville, an aristocratic Englishman of varied interests and a friend of Joseph Banks, was the first Westerner to flower tree peonies—which he did in his garden near Paddington, in the late 1790s. One of these early flowers was described as being very double and magenta in color, fading to a lighter shade at the outer edge of the petals.

In 1802 a plant was brought to England from China by a Captain James Prendergast on his ship *Hope*. Its flower was described as being a semi-double white, with purple spots at the base of the petals, considered by botanists to be the true wild species, one of the ancestors of the moutans. They first named it *Paeonia papaveracea*. Later this was changed to *P. moutan papaveracea*; now it seems to be considered as a subspecies of *P. rockii*. Only much later did tree peonies become more generally available in European nurseries, largely thanks to the efforts of Robert Fortune, who first set sail from England for China in 1843—commissioned to seek a blue peony ("the existence of which, however, is doubtful") among other things. Robert Fortune made four trips in all to China and was responsible for introducing many plants to the Western world, including 25 fine varieties of Chinese tree peonies—but no blue-flowered plants. That remains an elusive goal. 'Bijou de Chusan', a tree peony still known and grown today, was first introduced by Fortune.

By the end of the 19th century nurseries in Holland, France and Belgium were propagating numerous varieties of tree peonies, either from imported Chinese plants or from seed. Many of them were of poor quality, with big heavy flowers that hung down among the foliage. Much confusion existed about the origin and correct naming of them. No one seemed to know where any species came from until 1910, when plant-hunter William Purdom found in western China a bushy tree peony that bore muddy red flowers. He sent a herbarium specimen to the Arnold Arboretum at Harvard University, and this plant was subsequently named *Paeonia suffruticosa* var. *spontanea*.

In 1914, Reginald Farrer found plants of a wild white variety in Gansu near the Chinese border with Tibet, and he later described the find in his book *On the Eaves of the World*. He had climbed to a tiny mountain village and was exploring the wooded hills nearby in the evening. He talks about his excitement in seeing the plant from afar, yet not believing it could really be a flower, because of its size, until he came close enough to see in all its glory "that single enormous blossom, waved and crimped into the boldest grace of line, of absolute pure white, with featherings of deepest maroon radiating at the base of the petals from the boss of golden fluff at the flower's heart."

About a decade later, Joseph Rock, an Austrian-American explorer, geographer, linguist and botanist who spent most of his time in the period 1922–49 studying the flora, peoples and languages of southwest China and eastern Tibet, rediscovered a spectacular plant answering to the same description, in a lamasery in Gansu. Believing it to be a wild rather than a cultivated peony, he collected seeds from it and took them to the West. Plants were raised from this seed in Europe and North America. It is Rock's name that is now used to describe this plant, the species *Paeonia rockii*, originally named *P. suffruticosa* 'Rock's Variety' or *P. suffruticosa* 'Joseph Rock'.

Japanese tree peonies

The origin of Japanese tree peonies is similar to that of the Chinese varieties. It is believed that there are no tree peonies endemic to Japan and that they arrived there about the seventh century, brought by Buddhist monks along with various fruit trees such as apple and apricot. Although Westerners reported seeing tree

TOP: A newly opened tree peony catches the morning light.

MIDDLE: With pink stems and pink reflections in the leaves, this tree peony could win a fashion award for color coordination.

ABOVE: Once this glorious tree peony would have been called a variety of *Paeonia suffruticosa*. A more recent classification has changed the species name to *P. rockii*.

peonies blooming in Japan in both the 17th and 18th centuries, there is no record of their being imported to the West until 1844, when a collection from the Imperial Gardens of Tokyo and Kyoto was shipped to a nursery in Holland. Little is known about the fate of these plants, and it was not until 50 years later that Japanese varieties in appreciable numbers found their way to Europe and the United States, being exported directly from Japanese nurseries. These plants were all grafted onto a moutan with a poor habit and tended to be short-lived, although they did set fertile seed, which was used to produce new plants.

To add to the difficulties of would-be growers, the naming of plants that came from Japan in the early years of the 20th century was imprecise, and difficulties arose because of translation problems and inaccurate catalogue lists.

By the 1950s, with the help of the American Peony Society and the work of several U.S. breeders, some order had been created out of chaos. It became possible to buy some of the best Japanese varieties in the United States, with the assurance that each plant would match its description.

In later years the Japanese have grafted their tree peonies onto herbaceous peony stock. So long as they are planted deeply enough so the scion can gradually produce its own roots, these plants become established much more reliably than their predecessors.

The Japanese, in their development of the tree peony, favored a simpler flower than their Chinese counterparts, with flowers being mainly single or semi-double. Their double flowers are not as heavy as the Chinese varieties and the stems support the flowers more strongly. They also seed more freely than the Chinese plants.

LEFT: 'Renkaku', also known as 'Flight of the Cranes', a perennially popular tree peony. *RIGHT:* Japanese tree peony 'Choyjeraku'.

Major modern developments

A major event in the development of future tree peonies occurred in the later decades of the 19th century, when the French Jesuit priest, Jean Marie Delavay, discovered in China the two species *Paeonia lutea* and *P. delavayi*, both of which bear flowers that are considerably different from those of the moutans. In the late 1880s he sent plants of both to Paris, where they bloomed several years later. Some botanists consider them to be the same species, and they are often listed as belonging to the Delavay Group. However, there is no confusing the flowers. Those of the plant usually called *Paeonia lutea* are small, single and clear yellow; those of *P. delavayi* are also small and single, but range from darkest maroon to a clear blood-red.

It wasn't long before these two species featured in the breeding program of Frenchman Victor Lemoine, one of the most significant European breeders at the end of the 19th century. He did a lot of work crossing Chinese forms of *Paeonia lactiflora*, and he was also the first to start cross-breeding with wild peonies. With his colleague, Professor Louis Henry, Lemoine experimented in crossing *Paeonia lutea* with some of the (moutan) varieties and, with his successes, introduced a true yellow into the coloring of tree peonies, thus laying the foundations for the U.S. cultivation of what was to become known as the "lutea hybrids."

Lemoine's cultivars such as 'Chromatella', 'Alice Harding', 'L'Esperance' and 'La Lorraine' are still on the market today, and they themselves have been used in subsequent breeding programs. In Japan they are sold under the following Japanese names: 'Kinshi' ('Chromatella'), 'Kinkou' ('Alice Harding'), 'Kintei' ('L'Esperance') and 'Kinyou' ('La Lorraine'). 'Souvenir du Professeur Maxime Cornu' ('Kinkaku' in Japan), one of the most beautiful hybrid tree peonies ever raised, is a lutea hybrid created by Professor Henry.

About the time of World War I, Professor A.P. Saunders in the United States, excited by the hybrids produced in France, procured plants of *P. lutea* and *P. delavayi* and immediately started experimenting with them in his breeding program. He saved the pollen of various moutan (*P. suffruticosa*) varieties, often using Japanese plants with single or semi-double flowers, and put it on the later-blooming *Paeonia lutea* and *P. delavayi*. The results were vigorous plants with large, well-formed and beautiful flowers held on strong stems in colors which vastly extended the range that had been previously possible. The first of these was 'Argosy', introduced in 1928, which produced bright yellow flowers. 'Banquet' followed, with bicolored red and yellow flowers. Saunders introduced more than 70 hybrid tree peonies, including yellows, ivory and mauve bicolors, dark maroons, and yellows suffused with rich red.

When the professor died in 1953, his assistant, William Gratwick in New York, continued to work with his cultivars, with the aim of creating tree peony hybrids that incorporated the best qualities of each of the moutan (*suffruticosa*) and the *Lutea* species. Moutan would contribute large flowers of elegant texture and strong stems to hold the flowers well while *Paeonia lutea* would add vigor, fine foliage and yellow coloring if desired.

Gratwick was later joined by his friend Nassos Daphnis, a distinguished artist of Greek birth who over a period of 50 years also produced some ravishing tree peony varieties. Continuing the trend started by the French breeder Lemoine and carried on by Professor Saunders, he made crosses using *Paeonia lutea* and *P. delavayi* and selected moutan varieties, always with a view to combining the vitality of the species with the beauty of the moutans. Although he produced hundreds of new flowers, he registered only those he considered extraordinarily beautiful. Many he created displayed bold new colors, such as 'Boreas', a dark burgundy-red; 'Leda', which is an unusual combination of mauve, pink and plum; and 'Zephyrus', a mixture of pink and peach with ruby flares. He gave all his creations recognized Greek names. (For details of more named tree peony cultivars, see Appendix 1 at the end of the book.)

OPPOSITE: 'Boreas', a hybrid tree peony bred by Nassos Daphnis.

BELOW: Hybrid tree peony 'Golden Pleasure'.

BOTTOM: 'Black Panther' is a favorite tree peony hybrid created by the famous American hybridizer Professor A.P. Saunders.

What are tree peonies?

The name "tree peony" is misleading—"shrub" or "bush" would be a better description. In contrast to the herbaceous varieties, tree peonies do not disappear underground and hibernate for the winter. As does any deciduous shrub, they lose their leaves and the woody structure remains, growing sturdier as the years pass, though rarely attaining a height of more than 8 ft. (2.4 m). Most grow about 4 ft. (1.2 m) tall and similarly wide.

Tree peonies can live to a great age and, although they may seem very expensive at the outset, are well able to outlive the gardener who plants them. Some plants in China are reputed to be 200 years old.

The flowers are frequently bigger than those on their herbaceous cousins and they range in color through maroon, crimson, scarlet and various shades of pink, to pure white. There are also tree peonies with yellow or purple flowers and yet others where any of the foregoing colors may be paired. This amazing range is surprising when it is realized that they originate from very few species.

Their flowering season is not long—usually from late April to late May (or early October to early November in the Southern Hemisphere)—but the sight of a mature tree peony in full bloom is memorable. It may have in excess of 100 flowers, and these can be 10 in. (25 cm) or more across.

Once the blooms have faded the shrub is attractive through summer because of its interesting foliage, which differs from variety to variety. Some plants display foliage that is fine, lacy and light green; others have dark green leathery leaves that are deeply dissected and sit on the shrub like giant, spread-out hands. When the seedpods develop they add yet another dimension, and in autumn some of the leaves turn rich purple; yet others are red or golden.

These shrubs do need cherishing. Michael Haworth-Booth reminds his readers that a tree peony, unlike a rhododendron or an azalea, does not look after itself: "It has to have any dead bits of growth removed from time to time and it may require careful watering in a particularly dry spell. Furthermore it is easily killed by being trodden on by jobbing gardeners, blundered into by clumsy dogs or bashed with sticks by wild children."

Many tree peonies bred in China have names that sound impossibly romantic when they are translated into English. 'Sheng Dan Lu', for example, translates as 'Taoist Stove Filled with the Pills of Immortality'—maybe because it is outsize in all respects. The flowers are very big and filled with crimson-pink petals, both small and large, and the plant can grow as tall as 10 ft. (3 m). Then there is 'Wu Long Peng Sheng', which translates to either 'Black Dragon Holds a Splendid Flower' or 'Precious Offering from the Black Snake'. This has dark magenta-red petals.

Climate and conditions

The tree peony is an adaptable plant. It is extremely hardy and will live in cold northern climates (zone 4, although some protection from freezing winter winds is necessary), in warmer climates (zone 9 with some shade), and anywhere in between.

Nor is it too fussy about soil. Sand or clay, acid or alkaline, the tree peony will still flourish, but it prefers a fertile, well-drained soil with a pH of between 6 and 7. If your soil is either heavy clay or fine sand, it needs to have plenty of organic, humus-rich material added to it to increase the fertility and break up the clay. Gypsum or copious amounts of sand are also effective for separating clay particles, making it more plant-friendly and allowing it to drain freely. If water pools in heavy clay conditions, your plant could eventually drown. Tree peonies need to be planted deeply to thrive, and their roots like to burrow down into good, friable soil.

Once established, tree peonies are drought-tolerant plants, though some watering in summer is necessary in low-rainfall areas. Don't be tempted to water them until the soil is actually dry below the surface, and then let them dry out between waterings. Planting them within range of an automatic watering system is not a good idea. Above all, excellent drainage is very important.

These peonies need to be sheltered from strong winds, but some air movement helps to prevent fungal diseases like peony wilt. Given shade during the heat of the day, their blooms will last longer.

While no amount of cold will harm the tree peony while it is still dormant, the plant begins to grow as soon as spring is in the air. Young developing buds can be damaged by frost if they are exposed to morning sunshine too early. The shoots need to thaw gradually.

BELOW: As well as beautiful blooms, tree peonies have a structural character.

ABOVE: Hybrid tree peony 'Royal Sovereign'.

Planting and cultivation

Bare-root tree peonies can be planted in well-prepared ground in early spring so long as the earth is not frozen. The planting hole needs to be large, with the soil prepared in a wide enough area beyond the initial root-ball to allow the roots to spread easily. Add a few handfuls of bone meal, a general fertilizer or well-rotted garden compost or manure, and mix it with some of the removed soil to make a mound in the center of the hole. Plant the tree peony with its roots spread over the mound. Firm the soil around the roots, fill the hole, water the plant and firm the soil one more time to eliminate any air pockets around the roots.

Although plants sourced from China are most often grown on their own roots, those from other sources—Europe, Japan or North America—are usually grafted on to herbaceous peony stock. These specimens need to be planted deeply, with the graft union at least 4 in. (10 cm) below the soil to allow the tree peony (scion) to form its own roots above the graft and below the soil surface. In time, these take the place of the herbaceous roots and ensure the long life of the tree peony.

Pot-grown specimens from a nursery should be planted in the ground slightly deeper than the soil level in the container. Those bought from garden centers and nurseries are usually three to four years old and should flower the year after planting.

Sometimes a newly planted tree peony will appear to make little growth in its first season, but it is probably busily developing a solid root base underground. If the foliage looks reasonably healthy, all is going well. Occasionally the main stem may die back a little. Don't stress! Next spring vigorous growth will most likely shoot from the lower part of the stem or even from below soil level.

If your plant is grafted, look out for suckers from the herbaceous rootstock. You will recognize them by their foliage, which is quite different from the tree peony foliage. Cut them off at ground level. If they are not removed, the herbaceous stock will eventually take over from the graft and you will lose your tree peony.

Feeding

Tree peonies are heavy feeders. Summer is a time of storing up energy in the roots and in late summer the plants will make buds for next season. To encourage flowering in the following spring, apply a generous top-dressing every autumn of blood, fish and bone or a slow-release organic fertilizer with a low nitrogen and high potash content.

Pruning

These are shrubs that respond well to judicious pruning. The aim is to create and maintain a voluminous bush with lots of stems that, preferably, will not need staking.

In late winter, just as the growth buds are swelling, get rid of any dead wood, but check carefully before you lop off the whole branch—sometimes new shoots appear lower down the stem, even when the upper part of the branch is dead. Prune the dead parts back to the new bud. Whole branches will sometimes die. These should be pruned back to just above ground level. (Stark dead branches among glorious spring blooms create a bad hair day.)

BELOW: Tree peony bloom ready to open.

Don't be tempted to prune any plants that are less than three years old unless there is dead wood that needs removing. After this, if your plant has few stems and is poorly shaped, then discipline it firmly, pruning it back to any buds that are forming at the base of the stems, or to shoots coming from below the soil.

Early spring is the best time to prune, even if it does mean sacrificing some flowers in the coming year. If you prune after flowering, regrowth is slower—and the aim in the first few years is to establish a tree that is well shaped and strong.

When your tree peony has been growing for several years, it may benefit from a thinning of the interior branches. This will allow the shrub to put its energies into flowering rather than excessive leaf production. It will also allow more air and light to circulate, reducing the chance of fungus attack.

If you inherit an older tree peony that has been neglected, it can be transformed by severe pruning. It is best to work around the tree systematically, cutting back one main stem each year to about 6 in. (15 cm). It takes courage, but the results are usually successful.

The shape of the bush can be changed by pruning the top bud from the tallest branch. This will cause more branches to grow from older branches or the trunk, and will eventually create a bushier shrub. Occasionally, after a severe winter, several top branches will die back. But if the tree is healthy and has been planted deeply enough, new sprouts will come up from the ground.

The rough bark on the stems of an established plant can be attractive, and if you want to enjoy its texture you can prune out leaf buds low to the ground. This system of pruning would suit a single specimen planted in a Japanese-style garden.

If huge flowers are what you want, bud thinning can be carried out at the same time as pruning. To do this, only one strong, healthy shoot is kept on each branch, although on vigorous varieties more buds can be retained to increase the number of flowers and to prolong the flowering period.

Species ancestors

Formerly regarded as separate species, the following four plants are now grouped together by some botanists and considered variations of one species: *P. delavayi*, *P. lutea*, *P. potaninii*, and *P. lutea* var. *ludlowii*, a similar plant to *P. lutea* but larger and more spectacular in all its parts.

The peony formerly called *Paeonia suffruticosa* or moutan peony has been divided, in the new botanical classification, into the following different species: *Paeonia decomposita* (syn. *P. szechuanica*), *Paeonia jishanensis*, *Paeonia ostii*, *Paeonia quii*, *Paeonia rockii*, and *Paeonia yananensis*.

OPPOSITE (from top): 'Lemon Drops', 'Perfection', 'Flashlight' and 'Clarity'.
ABOVE: Last year's seedpods stay on the tree for a long time. Those of *Paeonia lutea* var. *ludlowii* are shown here.

9 Tree Peonies in the Garden

The tree peony is a spectacular flowering shrub that is often overlooked when gardeners are planning for spring. It is easy to concentrate on bulbs and spring blossoms like viburnums and flowering cherries, and then move directly on to thinking about summer-blooming plants. However, tree peonies fill a gap when the first flush of spring is fading and the rhododendrons and roses are not yet in their full splendor. These plants enjoy a wide range of climatic conditions, are tolerant of limey soil and do not take up a lot of space—an important consideration in today's small gardens. Tree peonies are also plants that are better enjoyed at close quarters, another reason to grow one or more in small areas.

Site selection

Every plant does better if it likes its situation. Tree peonies are no different, but choosing a position that is best suited to your tree peony will depend on your climate. Generally speaking, tree peonies need at least half a day's sunshine followed by some afternoon shade. However, where conditions are often cloudy and wet, they need all the sunlight they can possibly get and should be planted in full sun. Where sunlight and temperatures can be extreme for most of the summer, the plants prefer dappled shade to protect them from sunburn. And tree peonies will perform better if they have protection from strong winds, especially in areas where severe freezing gales are common in winter.

OPPOSITE: Tree peony 'Guest of Honour'.

RIGHT: This tree peony was taken as a divison from a neglected farm garden nearly 60 years ago.

TOP: Looking like a tree peony, 'Morning Lilac' is in fact an intersectional hybrid.

ABOVE: A tree peony in full bloom, showing off its *Paeonia rockii* ancestry. (Formerly it would have gone by the name *P. suffruticosa*).

The wall of a house or shed can offer shelter; a fence or a group of evergreen trees close by would also provide asylum. Some growers resort to erecting a temporary buffer by wrapping a burlap bag around the tree peony branches and stuffing it with straw, or erecting a wire cage filled with leaves or straw. It's important, though, to remove these in late winter as the shrub may be tempted to break into bud abnormally early. Placing mulch around young tree peonies in zone 6 or below also offers some protection. Don't let water from heavy rains or thawing snow pool around the plant for any length of time. Remember, excellent drainage is always necessary and friable soil helps to ensure this.

In warm climates—zone 9—tree peonies may need to be fooled into dormancy. To do this, strip off all the leaves in November or early December (May or early June in the Southern Hemisphere) and don't provide any water for these two months. The plant then believes it is wintering over and readies itself for the coming spring.

Most Chinese tree peonies bloom in their fifth year, although occasionally plants bloom a year earlier—when the flowers tend to be immature in size and shape. They do require some patience. Some extremely slow varieties (such as 'Pea Green', still grown but known to have been in cultivation a thousand years ago in China) do not bloom until their eighth year. Remember, tree peonies can live for over a hundred years, so even a five-year-old plant is still a baby.

Designing with tree peonies

From a landscape designer's point of view, a tree peony has several outstanding characteristics. What other shrub produces such mouthwatering flowers so early in the season, especially in cold climates? What other shrub lives for so long with similarly little maintenance? And what other single plant can create the exotic ambience that one tree peony lends to an enclosed garden or any sliver of outdoor space?

Plants with attitude

Tree peonies were never meant by nature to be shy, retiring, back-of-the-border subjects. Nor were they meant to be submerged among bigger, more vigorous shrubs. A mature tree peony, at the height of the flowering season, is a wonder to behold. The flowers are bigger than the biggest rose, opulent yet fragile, and composed of such complicated colorings that often it is impossible to describe them satisfactorily. If any flower was meant to be oohed and aahed over, the tree peony bloom is it.

But the plants offer more than just magical flowers. Tree peonies provide changing interest all year round—an important feature in small gardens, where there is no tolerance for nonperformers. Once the flowers are over, their foliage is attractive—both in summer when it is textured and green, and in autumn

when it turns fiery. Winter comes and the leaves disappear, but the framework remains as a silhouette.

These shrubs need to be planted where they can shine—in front of solid evergreen trees, for example, or in small groups beside tall slender trees such as cypresses, which accent their fullness. Plant several tree peonies near the front of a perennial border, where they can create a splash in spring. As with herbaceous peonies, add some spiky-leafed plants beside them, to contrast with their lush foliage. Roses nearby could act as complementary stars after the peonies have flowered.

In an intimate design—beside an entryway, at the corner of the house or veranda, in a small courtyard—a single plant can be used as a focal point. If there is a wall behind it to show off the foliage, so much the better. For spring drama, try planting two matching plants, one either side at the top of a flight of garden steps. At the bottom, place a pair of a later-flowering variety.

In a shrubbery, tree peonies add volume, and because of their size can be used at the edge of a woodland planting, much like a rhododendron or azalea. Just make sure they have enough space to stand out. Remember, pale flowers will add light to a dark corner, whereas dark colors tend to be absorbed and merge into the background.

ABOVE: Tree peony 'Banquet' opens out into a glorious red semi-double bloom.

ABOVE LEFT: Tree peony
'Israel,' shaded like a
watercolor painting.
ABOVE RIGHT: Forget-
me-nots provide a
contrast at the feet
of the tree peony
'Superstition'.

If you have a gently sloping hillside that needs furnishing, then tree peonies cascading from top to bottom, interspersed with one or two groups of conifers for green foliage in winter, would create a spectacle. (Keep in mind that tree peonies need enough space to grow free of the roots of the taller trees.) In China, tree peonies have been grown in terraces for hundreds of years. As in a hillside planting, the effect of their flowers descending in tiers is spectacular. Grown in a raised terrace, tree peonies whose flowers tend to hang down can also be appreciated more easily.

In the South Island of New Zealand, a couple who export tree peonies have established a large garden that is a fine showplace for these plants. Bordered on three sides by a tall green hedge, interspersed with climbing roses and clematis, the tree peonies grow in raised beds, separated by bark paths. Each block is edged by the double-flowered *Arabis caucasica* 'Flore Pleno', which creates a frothing mass of white when the tree peonies are in flower. Forget-me-nots and corydalis ramble at the feet of the peonies, and their delicate blue flowers complement all the myriad shades that tree peonies produce. Several herbaceous peony seedlings are scattered at random among the tree peony beds to extend the flowering season; when the blooms are over, the tree peony foliage remains as blocks of textured green while the climbing roses around the border of the garden have their day. There are literally hundreds of tree peonies in this garden. Not many of us have this kind of space, but the same idea could be repeated on a smaller scale.

Several tree peonies can also be used as a low boundary planting or as a street edging. Remember that they are deciduous, with just their skeletons remaining in winter.

Tree peonies in pots

Unlike its cousin, the tree peony is quite happy to travel around. So long as there is no excessive damage to the roots when it is dug up, it is very tolerant of an itinerant lifestyle. This makes it an ideal plant for container growing as it can be repotted from time to time when it outgrows its home. It also means that it can be planted in a smaller container than a herbaceous variety, making it easier to move around for maximum effect in the garden—or for winter protection in areas below zone 7.

In both China and Japan, tree peonies have been grown in pots for centuries and are often used for indoor decoration or as objects of beauty in a courtyard. In Japan they are often brought inside when in flower, and placed in a position of importance, such as on a special dais, where they can be admired or gazed at in quiet contemplation.

In the West, tree peonies are not frequently seen as container subjects. However, growing to 3–4 ft. (1–1.2 m) tall in a pot and with deeply cut, attractive foliage and stunning flowers, these plants make an eye-catching feature, ideal for today's courtyard or patio, or placed one on either side of an entryway.

Their soil requirements in tubs are similar to those of their herbaceous cousins, but the potting mix must be especially porous—adding sand, fine gravel, ground pumice/perlite or well-rotted leaf mold will help to achieve this quality. (Note that the inclusion of peat may make the mix too acidic.) Tree peony roots need to breathe and the water needs to drain off quickly. The plants are greedy feeders, so make sure the mix is rich and that feeding continues through the season if you are using a liquid fertilizer.

Early autumn is the best time for potting tree peonies. The lower-growing, upright, strong, free-blooming varieties with many feeding roots are best for container culture. The species *P. lutea*, for example, would not be a good choice.

If you are potting up a plant from the garden, after digging, leave it out for a day or two to let it become limp for easy handling. Remove any damaged branches or any that are growing very closely together. Shorten very long roots to fit, place the plant in the pot and, as when planting tree peonies in the ground, make sure the grafting point is at least 4 in. (10 cm) below the surface of the soil. Firmly compact the mix. Water it well and place the potted tree peony where it will get at least four to five hours of sun.

When the plant is in bloom, remember that the flowers will last longer if they have shade for part of the day.

To keep them tidy, any excessively long shoots should be cut back once the plant has lost its leaves. In early spring give tree peonies protection from cold winds. If their shoots are frosted, they need shade from the sun until the frost has thawed.

BELOW: 'First Arrival', a modern tree peony.

ABOVE: Late-blooming 'Golden Bowl' is a Saunders's hybrid tree peony.

OPPOSITE: Corydalis makes an unexpected companion plant for a tree peony.

If your climate is harsh during the winter months, site the tub where the plant will get some protection. In severe conditions the root-ball needs extra insulation—an overcoat of straw maybe for the container, or a swaddling coat of thermal fabric or bubble wrap. If the pot is not too large, it can be sunk in the ground outside, with the plant exposed but covered if necessary. Where winters are excessively severe, tree peonies in pots should be overwintered inside—but not in heated accommodation.

Cricket Hill Nursery, a well-known peony specialist in Connecticut, suggests root-control bags as the best container for tree peonies. Made from a nonwoven plastic fabric that looks like felt, they are fast draining. Because they provide quick drainage and allow hair roots to grow through the sides of the bag, the roots are "pruned" by their exposure to air and are less inclined to girdle as they do in plastic or clay pots. The bag can be placed in a decorative pot, which of course must have good drainage.

An added advantage to these grow-bags is that they are lighter to move around than pots, especially if there is a need to bury them during winter. Where the ground freezes in winter, plants in these bags need to be insulated or stored at 35–40°F (1–4°C).

Left outside over early winter and then brought into an unheated greenhouse or indoors (where it is cool) in January (Northern Hemisphere; or July in the Southern Hemisphere), tree peonies will be encouraged to flower sooner. In *Peonies: The Imperial Flower*, Jane Fearnley-Whittingstall relates that tree peonies in China, intended to flower between December and April, are dug up 60–70 days before the flowering time, stripped of their leaves and aired for two days to soften their roots. They are then shipped to their destination and, about 50 days before their flowering date, are potted up. Even earlier flowering is induced by storing them at unnaturally cold temperatures; delayed flowering is manipulated by prolonging the dormant period.

I'm glad I'm not a tree peony in China.

Varieties of tree peonies recommended for container growing

'Beautiful Spring Red', 'Big Brown Purple', 'Big Deep Purple', 'Black Dragon Holds a Splendid Flower', 'Cao Zhou Red', 'Champion Pink', 'Cinnabar Rampart', 'Hu's Red', 'Lan Tian Jade', 'Lotus That Shines in the Sun', 'Luoyang Red', 'Necklace with Precious Pearls', 'Number Eighteen', 'Phoenix White', 'Purple Velvet', 'Shandong Pink', 'Silver Red', 'Twin Beauty', 'White Jade' and 'Zhao's Pink'.

10 Intersectional Hybrids

What are they?

This is certainly not a name dreamed up to entice gardeners, but it is a descriptive name, and it refers to the newest peony hybrid, which is actually a cross between the two sections of the genus—tree peonies and the herbaceous varieties. It is a cross that frustrated peony breeders for centuries. Even the famous American breeder Professor Arthur Saunders believed it to be an impossible dream and counted it as his major failure that he was unable to create one of these hybrids.

Eventually though, in Japan, the seemingly impossible happened. Nurseryman Toichi Itoh made a cross between the yellow tree peony 'Alice Harding' (originally produced by Lemoine as one of his *P. lutea* crosses) and the double, white-flowered herbaceous peony 'Kakoden'. Twenty-seven seedlings survived, all herbaceous in appearance. None of the seedlings bloomed until 1963 and by then, sadly, Toichi Itoh had died. But four of his plants produced deep yellow, double flowers of high quality.

Discovered several years later by an American peony grower, Louis Smirnow, they were imported into the United States, propagated and sold under the names of 'Yellow Crown', 'Yellow Dream', 'Yellow Emperor' and 'Yellow Heaven'.

Following this success, several American hybridizers have followed in the

OPPOSITE: Intersectional hybrid 'Hillary'.

RIGHT: 'Callie's Memory' is an intersectional hybrid.

ABOVE LEFT: 'Yellow Dream', one of the earliest intersectional peonies.

ABOVE RIGHT: Intersectional hybrid 'Morning Lilac'.

footsteps of Toichi Itoh, producing more of these hybrids in a wide range of shades that would not be obtainable in strictly herbaceous crosses, although yellow remains the most common color. Most of those available on the market come from Roger Anderson, who has produced plants in colors ranging through orange, yellow, red and lavender, including the popular lemon-yellow 'Bartzella'. Others come from Don Hollingsworth, who is recognized for his dark yellow hybrids 'Garden Treasure' and 'Border Charm'; and from William Seidl, who introduced the fuchsia-rose–colored 'Rose Fantasy'.

Known now as either "intersectional hybrids" or "Itoh hybrids," these peonies produce tree peony flowers and glossy foliage on plants that are herbaceous in habit and therefore are lower-growing than the tree peonies. The stems of the plants tend to become woody as they age but still need to be treated like herbaceous varieties that are cut down to the ground in autumn. Flowering time follows that of the tree peonies.

The best of them are vigorous, very winter hardy and perform well when properly planted in deep, fertile, somewhat heavy soil, and when provided with adequate moisture. For people in cold northern climates they provide great yellow-flowering peonies that are exceptionally hardy.

They are propagated by root division, and eyes need to be evident both on the crown and on the underground portion of the stems that are part of the division.

Unfortunately they remain rather specialized plants and tend to be expensive.

Selected intersectional hybrids

'Bartzella'. A gorgeous peony (which is also hugely expensive)—bred by Roger Anderson and registered in 1986. Like 'Garden Treasure', it has deep yellow flowers and a good fragrance.

'Border Charm'. Bred by Don Hollingsworth in 1984. Mid-season, single, yellow petals, paler at edges, large dusky flares at the base, medium-size flower. Stiff stems have a striking horizontal posture, making this an especially interesting choice for the position of a semi-prostrate shrub. Vigorous, prolific increase.

'Garden Treasure'. Bred by Don Hollingsworth in 1984. Mid-season, semi-double to nearly full double, petals open yellow-gold, lightly flared scarlet, fragrant. Extended flowering period—up to four weeks in cooler climates. Vigorous, medium height. Well-grown plants may form a 5 ft. (1.5 m) wide mound at maturity, yielding four to five dozen blossoms. American Peony Society Gold Medal Award, 1996.

'Lafayette Escadrille'. Bred by Pehrson/Seidl in 1989. Mid-season, single, dark red, smallish flower. Foliage much segmented, upright stems medium height, prolific multiplier. An interesting, smaller-scale novelty for the mixed border.

'Love Affair'. Bred by Don Hollingsworth (2005). Mid-season, semi-double, white, each flower a symmetrical bowl, mostly one per stem. This plant appeared as a mutation from the yellow-flowered 'Prairie Sunshine'. The two plants appear to be the same in all respects except the petal color and superior symmetry of this one—broad, rounded guard petals surround several rows of inner petals.

'Old Rose Dandy'. Bred by Laning in 1993. Mid-season, single, petals yellow-beige with purplish-rose blend at opening. The purplish pigments pale as the flower matures, though the underlying color remains. Prolific bloom with starlike flowers covering the rounded bush.

'Prairie Charm'. Bred by Don Hollingsworth in 1992. Mid-season, medium-large semi-double, clear yellow with a large red-purple flare at the base of each petal. All this encircles a prominent center of creamy-white and green. Dependable performer. Forms a substantial bush.

'Viking Full Moon'. Bred by Pehrson/Seidl in 1989. A single-flowered peony. Color is much paler than either 'Bartzella' or 'Garden Treasure', though still decidedly yellow.

BELOW: Intersectional hybrid 'Julia Rose'.

Peonies for Free

Peonies can become addictive. Plant one or two in your garden and it won't be long before you want a few more ... and then a few more again. Obviously you can keep buying plants, but you can also increase your stock of herbaceous peonies either by division or by collecting seeds and planting them. Tree peonies, however, are most often propagated by grafting.

Division of herbaceous peonies

If you are interested in fast results, division of the crown and rootstock is the best way to go. Each piece of crown that has a bud will grow and produce a plant of the same variety as the parent. This is the way that stocks of named varieties are built up.

Peonies don't take kindly to being dug up and moved but they will consent to being dug up and divided, provided they are big enough. It's best to wait until your bush has flowered for several seasons, though, before asking it to submit to being split up. Autumn is the optimum time for the operation. Cut down all the old stems to ground level but take care not to destroy the eyes, which usually form at the stem base of the current year's growth. Occasionally they form on the underground portion of some stems—so check for these before breaking or cutting the old stems away.

OPPOSITE: **Gorgeous antique shades, tree peony 'Composure'.**

RIGHT: **An anonymous** *Delavayi* **seedling with an attractive tawny coloring.**

If the soil is very dry, water your plant and allow a day before digging it out. Try not to damage the crown (central section), which is the "heart" of the plant and has power over the growth of roots and shoots. Include as many of the roots as possible; however, if the clump has been in place for many years, this will be difficult.

The roots are brittle when they are first dug, so it's a good idea to leave the exposed crown in the shade and covered—to prevent it from drying out—for a couple of days, until it becomes limp and therefore much easier to split into pieces.

Hose off all the surrounding soil to make it easier to see the material you are working with. Long roots that are awkward to deal with may need to be cut back to about 6 in. (15 cm). The size of the clump will determine how many clones it will give you, but each division needs to have plenty of root and at least one eye. If it contains three to five eyes it should flower in its second season. Sections with one eye will eventually flower, but they may take several years.

The divisions are best taken from the outer parts of the clump, especially if it has been in the ground for a long time, as the center of the crown may have deteriorated and contain few, if any, eyes. Plan where you want to make the cuts before you start; then, using a sharp spade or large knife, slice through the clump as cleanly as possible. The new divisions can be stored briefly so long as they are well protected by straw, peat moss or some other organic material that will prevent them from drying out and shrinking.

When planting them, make sure not to bury them too deeply—the crown should be no more than 2 in. (5 cm) below the surface of the soil.

BELOW: Cherry blossom and peonies—classic plants of spring.

BELOW RIGHT: A tree peony, pretty in pink.

Propagating tree peonies

Tree peonies, like herbaceous varieties, can be propagated by division, although many varieties produce only a single main root, making division impracticable. For those plants that do produce side shoots, the same process as that used for herbaceous peonies can be employed, except that the above-ground stems on each division should be cut back to only a few inches above ground. The roots are tough, long and cylindrical. Any damaged or broken ends may need to be cut off after the plant has been excavated. Unlike the roots of herbaceous peonies, they are not brittle.

Not trees in the true sense of the word, these plants will rarely grow from cuttings, and the most common method of vegetative propagation is by grafting. (Propagating by seed will not produce plants that are identical to the parent.) Most growers graft a tree peony scion (budded shoot) onto a herbaceous peony rootstock, as this method seems to produce a stronger plant. As the plant grows, however, it is important to ensure that the herbaceous stock does not overtake the tree peony. The grafted plant needs to be planted deeply enough— 4 in. (10 cm)—to allow the scion to develop its own roots. Once this happens, the herbaceous root material can be cut away. Similarly, any herbaceous shoots that appear above ground should be cut away to prevent them from swamping the scion.

Gladys McArthur, a former peony breeder in New Zealand whose name lives on in the herbaceous peony named after her, used to pile compost around the selected tree peony to encourage new growth to form at its base. After a couple of years, this new growth would occasionally form its own roots—and thus a new plant that could be separated from the parent. She found this method more effective than layering, which is not generally a reliable way of propagating tree peonies.

Seed beginnings

Any seed, no matter how small, is a treasure box packed with magic, a capsule full of promise and potential glory. However, growing peonies from seed is for those who know how to wait and are not easily discouraged; plants take between four and five years from seed to flower and once in bloom, the flower may well be disappointing.

This method is also for those who are curious and want to breed a "new" plant, and who have the patience and recording skills to effect the pollination by hand. Each plant produced by seed is a unique individual with its own set of genes. Species breed true to type, and their offspring will usually look the same as their parents. Hybrids (crosses between two species) and crosses between two different varieties do not breed true, and their progeny is an unknown quantity. Playing God with their pollen can become an obsessive interest.

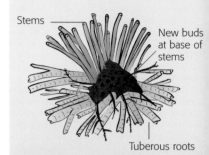

TYPICAL HERBACEOUS PEONY TUBEROUS ROOT CLUMP

Stems

New buds at base of stems

Tuberous roots

TOP: When dividing the crown to form new plants it is important to include one or two new buds as well as several tuberous roots in each separate division.

MIDDLE: Phormium makes an interesting companion plant for 'Coral Sunset'.

ABOVE: 'Coral Charm' flowers early in the season.

Some peonies, such as the species *Paeonia mlokosewitschii*, produce seeds of two different colors—bright coral red, and dark blue-black. Only the latter are fertile. All the species, however, are self-fertile, meaning that the pollen produced on one flower can fertilize other flowers on the same plant, thus giving the potential to produce lots of seeds. For this reason, commercial production of species seed is very successful.

Cultivars, however, come from a much greater variety of genes, and their fertility varies enormously. Fully double flowers don't produce seeds because their sexual parts have been transformed into extra petals.

All peony seeds have a double dormancy requirement, which means that first they require a period of warmth, during which a tiny root develops. Then they need a period of chilling before the shoot bursts through the skin of the seed. In a temperate climate, where the temperatures drop close to freezing or below, this will happen naturally if the seeds are planted out in the garden. In colder climates (zone 6 and lower), germinating the seeds indoors is a better option.

As soon as the seedpods open, collect the seed and sow it immediately if possible. The outer coating on the seed becomes harder over time, making germination more difficult; it can take as long as 18 months, or even more. Some growers rinse the seeds in a diluted bleach mixture or fungicide, to kill any bacteria that may infect the new plants.

Tree peony seeds, before they are fully ripe, are a mottled creamy-brown color. This is the time to collect them and sow them. Once they turn purplish-black they are most likely to be dormant. They germinate best in open ground in a semi-shady place, and it may take up to three years before they spring into action.

When sown outside in a cold frame or in a shady section of the garden, seed can produce a root within six weeks of sowing. The shoot will form in the next spring. If seeds are germinated in individual pots, it is a good idea to leave them undisturbed for two growing seasons. This will allow the roots to become well established before the trauma of being planted into a permanent position. Beware of moving small seedlings from shade to full sun—they will probably scorch.

If you want to germinate seed inside, the process imitates what happens in nature. Outdoors, the seeds ripen, drop to the ground and stay there through a period of warmth and usually some late summer or autumn rains. Winter comes, spring follows, the seeds germinate and the first leaves appear in spring.

TOP: Breaking out.

MIDDLE: Ripening seeds have their own beauty.

ABOVE: 'Roy Pehrson's Best Yellow', a herbaceous peony that is sometimes more ivory than yellow.

Indoors, the seeds need to be placed in a sealed plastic bag with some slightly moist vermiculite or sand. Stow the sealed bags somewhere warm, and check them frequently to ensure that the mix remains damp and to see when the root emerges. It may take several weeks or several months. When the roots are about 1 in. (2.5 cm) long, move the bag to a cool location. The temperature should be slightly above freezing.

In about 10 weeks the shoot should have appeared, and this is the time to pot seedlings up in containers, in seed-raising mix that is kept damp but not water-logged. Otherwise the seedlings will drown. Keep the seedlings indoors with some warmth until close to the end of summer, when they can be transferred to their permanent location in the garden. As with any other seedling, transfer them outside gradually to allow them to acclimatize.

Seeds of tree peonies, left to ripen on the bush, often produce little seedling trees that emerge around the parent in subsequent years. This happens especially with *Paeonia lutea* and *P. delavayi*.

Playing God

Home gardeners often find it intriguing to try to create their own "new" plants. It's a matter of keeping the bees away and intervening in the match-making process of the flowers. The excitement of breeding plants is in the lure of the unknown. Will the cross produce a magnificent, sought-after plant, or will it be an inconspicuous nonperformer? Assessing the qualities of the two parent plants helps to give some indication of what to expect. Dedicated breeders usually set out to produce a flower of a particular shape and color, or they may try to improve the foliage or form of a particular strain. The process from peony seed to flower takes at least five years, and then a further several years are needed before the mature flower, as well as the behavior of the whole plant, can be adequately assessed.

The skilled American artist-hybridizer Nassos Daphnis set out to create distinctive tree peonies that satisfied his own perception of beauty. Not only did he want to create a perfect flower, but he felt that the whole plant had to harmonize with nature and radiate a sense of calm and happiness for everyone who viewed it. Everything, including the plant's growing habit, leaves and structure, had to fulfill these criteria.

He made hundreds of crosses between moutan (or *suffruticosa*) varieties and *Paeonia lutea*. Unsurprisingly perhaps, relatively few of them attained his ideal of perfection. He named those that did, and all his creations display a flower with a beautiful center, surrounded by harmoniously arranged petals.

The process of cross-pollination for Daphnis was made more complicated by the fact that the two types of plants he worked with come into flower at different times. It was a matter of collecting the pollen from selected moutan plants and drying it to preserve it until the mother plants of the *Paeonia lutea* were just about to open their flowers. To prevent the *Paeonia lutea* flowers from self-pollinating, the petals of the opening buds and the immature anthers were then removed, leaving only the carpels and the stigma, which was not yet receptive to pollination and had to be covered to prevent possible cross-pollination by bees. Two or three days later, when the stigma became moist—indicating its readiness to receive the pollen—he placed the pollen on the stigma and once again covered it to ensure the integrity of his cross. He then had to await autumn, and hopefully the ripening of the seed thus formed.

Less experienced hybridizers find it simpler to work initially with two varieties of peonies that flower simultaneously. The pollen can then be removed from the "father" (or pollen parent) and put on the stigma of the "mother" (or pod parent) on the same day. Precautions against contamination from bees need to be taken, and it is also important to record the names of the parent plants and the dates on which the pollination took place. After that it is a matter of waiting and hoping.

12 Peonies on Display

While peonies in the garden make a spectacular sight when they are in flower, many varieties also make excellent cut flowers. Herbaceous peonies are becoming increasingly popular in the commercial cut-flower markets around the world. Growers and florists alike appreciate the fact that peonies travel well and remain in bud for a long time, making them an easy product to package and move around. Buyers love the opulence of the blooms as well as their long-lasting qualities.

Writing in an issue of the *American Peony Society Bulletin*, peony breeder Don Hollingsworth highlights the flowers' ability to stay fresh for extended periods. While packing blooms to take with him to an exhibition some years ago, he overlooked flowers of his home-bred double hybrid 'Many Returns', which had been cut in mid-May and refrigerated. When he eventually took them out of cold storage in late June and put them in a vase, they lasted for six days.

The secret to their long-lasting ability, especially if they are to make a journey, is in picking them at the right stage—too early, and they won't open; too late, and they won't travel well. Knowing when to harvest peonies is an art that develops from practice. Commercial growers pick the stems when the bud is well developed but still firm, and put them in cool storage as quickly as possible—ideally at 32°F (0°C)—where they will last for up to six weeks. Once

OPPOSITE: **Free to a good home.**
RIGHT: **Ready for market.**

ABOVE: **Sunset comes indoors.**

ABOVE RIGHT: **Thoroughly modern misses.**

they have arrived at their destination and been taken out of the refrigerator, stems in bud that are to be kept for any length of time should be stored in cool, clean water to which a drop of chlorine bleach or other flower preservative has been added. The buds need to be moistened occasionally with a fine spray. This water dissolves the sugars produced by the buds, which would otherwise dry out and be prevented from opening completely.

Flower buds that are loose and soft on purchase, with the color of the flower clearly recognizable, will bloom when they are put in water. Buds that show no color and feel hard are not likely to open.

The most important criteria when selecting varieties to grow for the market are larger flowers, unusual colors, high production and good flowering once they are removed from cool storage.

As in all fashion industries, trends in colors come and go. For the last few years peonies in shades of coral have been extremely popular. 'Coral Charm', 'Coral Supreme' and 'Coral Sunset', all developed in the 1960s and bearing big flowers that fade gently from their original coral pink to varying shades of cream or lemony-cream, have been big sellers. 'Sarah Bernhardt', a *Paeonia lactiflora* cultivar with double pink flowers, bred as long ago as 1906, is at the time of writing one of the biggest sellers on the Dutch market, followed by bright pink 'Dr. Alexander Fleming', cerise-red 'Karl Rosenfeld', and white 'Shirley Temple'. 'Red Charm', a deep crimson flower of bomb form, is a consistently good seller. In the United States and Canada, red and white peonies are always sought for the Christmas season. True yellow peonies are not numerous yet but are becoming increasingly popular, and breeders are working on producing a true orange bloom for the cut-flower market.

Cutting the flowers

When you cut peonies for the house, pick the flowers preferably in the evening, when they are at the "soft bud" stage—think of soft marshmallows—and leave at least three leaves on the stem on the plant. Recutting the stems under warm water prevents an air bubble from developing at the end of the stem, which can inhibit the uptake of water. Strip the lower leaves from the stems, and if possible leave your flowers standing in a bucket of water overnight. The flowers will last for up to 10 days in water if the stems are cut just as the round, ball-like buds begin to show true color. If they are cut at the fully open stage, they will last about five days.

Double varieties most often have a longer vase life than single flowers and, obviously, varieties with strong stems are easier to arrange than those with big flowers and weak stems. Tree peony blooms in general have shorter stalks than their cousins and sit more easily in shallow containers. Some of their flowers display such complex coloring that a single bloom, enhanced with foliage, is all it takes to create an arrangement. And don't forget about the seedpods when it comes to interesting autumn indoor arrangements.

In any one season at least half the blooms from a herbaceous peony should be left on the plant. Tree peonies should never be cut below the fourth leaf axil on any stem, as this may prevent that shoot from flowering the following season.

Any gardener who wishes to decorate the house for the whole peony season needs to do some planning at the planting stage. For a list of peonies that produce good cutting blooms from early to late season, see Appendix 1, page 134.

Dried flower routines

For those who like dried flowers, peonies are an excellent choice. Large double varieties, dried, remain relatively voluminous and many retain their bright colors. Reds and dark pinks are particularly successful. For drying purposes, the flowers are best cut when fully open (but before they start to fade), and when the foliage is dry. If the stems are cut long enough they can be tied in bunches and hung upside down in a warm, dark, airy space. Come winter, when the plants have retired underground, dried blooms used as indoor decoration remind us of their garden glory.

TOP: Fields of 'Coral Sunset' in New Zealand.

ABOVE: Peonies in profusion.

13 Troubleshooting

Both tree peonies and the herbaceous varieties have a reputation for being trouble-free plants, just so long as they are grown in an appropriate climate and provided with good drainage. As always, of course, plants that are well cared for and cherished are less likely to succumb to disease than those that are neglected. It's true for children, and it's true for plants.

Herbaceous peonies

In general, peonies are subject to few diseases, although botrytis is a recurring problem if the weather turns cold and excessively wet. Planting with sufficient space between individual plants enables good air circulation, which in turn discourages fungal attack.

Good hygiene in autumn is a sensible precaution. When the stems are cut down they should be burned to destroy any lurking spores. If botrytis has been a problem in the preceding season, it might be wise to dig out some of the soil around the base of the plant and replace it with a sterilized mix.

Botrytis and other fungal problems

If botrytis is a recurring problem, copper fungicide sprays can be used in spring when the new growth appears through the ground, then applied two weeks later and again in four weeks.

OPPOSITE: It's not hard to keep peonies looking as healthy as this example of the herbaceous peony 'Flame'.

RIGHT: 'Marie Fischer' opens blush pink and gradually turns to white.

Botrytis cinerea **or gray mold** can strike peonies in humid weather or when a plant has been fed too much nitrogenous fertilizer and the stems are weak and "sappy." If your plant shows evidence of gray mold on the stems or leaves and a dusty cloud of spores float into the air when the foliage is touched, then the disease has hit. Plants growing in badly drained soil are more likely to contract the disease. Prevention is always more effective than a cure, so move the plant if necessary, make sure there is plenty of space for air to circulate around it and avoid overfeeding with manure or other rich fertilizers.

Botrytis paeoniae **or botrytis blight** usually attacks the plant at the base of its leaves and flower stems. An ugly patch of soft brown tissue appears just above ground level. This later turns rather gray, and brown spots may appear on the leaves as the plant puts on spring growth. Later the buds will also be affected and will fall off. It's a nasty disease! Cold, wet weather is the main culprit. As soon as any shoots show signs of drooping, they need to be cut away at soil level. The foliage should then be sprayed with a copper-lime mixture.

Cladosporium paeoniae, **red spot or peony measles** is a fungal disease that causes purple spots to appear on leaves, stems, flower buds and petals. As with botrytis, providing healthy growing conditions is the best mode of attack.

Phytophthora cactorum **or downy mildew blight** is another nasty fungal disease that is similar to botrytis, though it often causes more damage. It tends to attack the leaves and stems, causing everything above to turn dark brown and collapse. Remove any shoots as soon as the telltale signs appear, and spray the plant with a copper-based fungicide.

Insects and other pests

As with most plants, peonies are occasionally subject to attack by insects or other pests.

Aphids spread viral disease. Although peony foliage is not one of their main targets, they may appear from time to time, especially on new shoots. A sharp blast from a hose on successive days should deter these pests. If this is not successful, try spraying on the following organic mix. Simmer 1 pound (0.5 kg) chopped rhubarb leaves in 2½ pints (1.5 L) of water for 30 minutes. Strain the mixture and store it in a glass jar. When ready to use, add 1 fluid ounce (28 mL) of dishwashing liquid to 2½ pints (1.5 L) of water and combine this with the rhubarb extract.

Slugs are another universal munching pest that will happily attack the new shoots as they push through the soil. Damaged stems may prevent flowering, so

OPPOSITE TOP: Species peonies, such as *P. emodi*, are generally trouble-free plants.

OPPOSITE MIDDLE: Tree peony 'First Arrival'.

OPPOSITE BOTTOM: Healthy foliage is necessary for the plant to look its best right through summer. The leaves of this tree peony, with their fernlike quality, are a design feature in themselves.

it's important to get rid of the slugs. Pellets laid around the plants work well; just make sure they are pet friendly.

Ants often crawl into the flowers for a feast of nectar but cause no harm.

Wireworms can be troublesome, especially in a garden that has been newly dug from grass cover. The grubs look like short lengths of orange wire and they will eat the plants around the crown, often severing roots completely. If your peony dies for no apparent reason, check the roots. If evidence is found of wireworm, the soil may need to be treated. Just remember if you use a general soil sterilizer, the "goodies" will be killed along with the "baddies."

No flowers on your plants? Check the following list:
- **Plants too young.** Some varieties are slow to mature.
- **Planted too deep.** Crown should be no more than 2 in. (5 cm) below the ground, with buds facing upward.
- **Divisions without any eyes planted.**
- **Spindly thin stems and sparse flowers.** Clump may need dividing or feeding, or moving to a better location.
- **Buds blackening.** May be due to late frost or botrytis attack after heavy rains.
- **No buds.** Plants may be undernourished. Feed with balanced fertilizer.
- **Ground too dry.** Water newly planted areas well and continue for the first year.
- **Soft growth and sparse, poor flowers.** An oversupply of nitrogen.

Tree peonies
Tree peonies are even more trouble-free than their cousins, but they are still subject to **botrytis attack** in unfavorable weather conditions. Treatment is the same as for the herbaceous varieties.

Sudden-death disease is just that. Stems wilt very quickly and need to be removed immediately, at below-ground level. If the disease is caught quickly, the plant should live and send out new growth.

Rose borer can be a problem. You will know about its presence if you find minuscule holes in older branches in which eggs have been laid. A narrow wire, inserted in the hole and twisted around, should kill the larvae.

Occasionally, tree peonies will suffer from **chlorosis**, a problem caused by lack of iron and evident when leaves turn yellow but the veins remain green. This problem will affect the growth of the plant and can be remedied by treating the soil with a preparation that contains iron. Seek advice from your garden center.

Appendix 1: Selected Peony Varieties

Selected herbaceous peony varieties

The following lists are by no means comprehensive. Their purpose is to give gardeners who are new to peonies some guidance in choosing plants that answer their particular needs. Remember that seasons vary from country to country, from micro-climate to micro-climate. Early, mid-season and late are indications only of flowering time. They cannot be definitive. Sense of fragrance is also variable and always a personal reaction.

Anemone varieties and some special characteristics

Cultivar name	Guard petals	Center	Season
'Bowl of Beauty'	pink guard petals	cream-yellow staminodes	mid–late
'Golden Dawn'	ivory-white petals	pale yellow	mid
'Instituteur Doriat'	carmine-red petals	pinkish-carmine petalodes, tipped white	late
'Pink Lemonade'	soft pink petals	yellow	mid
'Powder Puff'	pink petals	cream	mid
'Prairie Afire'	pink petals	fiery-red petalodes	mid
'Primevere'	creamy-white petals	sulfur yellow	mid

Japanese varieties and some special characteristics

Cultivar name	Guard petals	Center	Season
'Ama-No-Sode'	pinky-lilac	pale gold	mid
'Barrington Belle'	rose-red golden margins	red, bright	mid
'Bride's Dream'	creamy-white	soft yellow to cream	late
'Charles Burgess'	deep crimson	burgundy, light golden	mid
'Cheddar Supreme'	milky-white	gold	mid
'Chocolate Soldier' (*P. lactiflora* x *P. officinalis*)	dark red-brown	golden	early
'Do Tell'	orchid-pink	pink, wine-red and gold	early–mid
'Fancy Nancy'	cerise pink	lacy pink	mid
'Gay Paree'	dark cerise	creamy-tinted	mid
'Globe of Light'	rosy-pink	pale gold	mid–late
'Glowing Candles'	pale pink	creamy-beige	mid
'Hot Chocolate'	deep red	red and gold	mid
'Isani-guidi'	dazzling white	rich buff	mid
'King of England'	cerise-pink	gold-streaked dark pink	mid–late
'Kukenu-jishia'	light pink with rose shading	light gold	mid–late
'Largo'	rose-pink	vibrant rose and gold	mid
'Leto'	pure white to white	rich yellow fading	early–mid
'Mandarin's Coat'	deep rose-pink	yellow	early–mid
'Mikado'	dark crimson	butter yellow	mid–late
'Plainsman'	pale pink to ivory-white	yellow-white	mid–late
'Snow Swan'	smooth petaled white	rose and gold	mid
'Sword Dance'	bright red	rose and gold	mid
'White Sands'	many-petaled white	yellow, fragrant	mid

Early-flowering varieties

'America'	single, fiery-red with golden center tuft
'Avante Garde' (*P. lactiflora* x *P. wittmanniana*)	single, large, pale rose-pink with darker veins, red stem; tall
'Blaze'	single, true red with rounded petals, sunny-yellow center
'Buckeye Belle'	semi-double, dark red, dramatic
'Burma Ruby '	single, deep red, fragrant (early–mid)

Some modern yellow-colored American hybrid peonies

'Claire de Lune'
'Daystar'
'Early Glow'
'Goldilocks'
'Haung Jin Lun'
'Lemon Chiffon'
'Nova and Nova II'
'Prairie Moon'
'Summer Glow'

'Coral Charm'	semi-double, coral-pink fading to peachy-cream, gold center
'Coral Sunset'	semi-double, coral-pink fading to pale lemon
'Coral Supreme'	a looser double than the preceding two flowers
'Cytherea' (*P. lactiflora* x *P. peregrina*)	cup-shaped, semi-double, rose-pink; dense foliage, good cut, flower (early–mid)
'Early Windflower' (*P. emodi* x *P. veitchii*)	white, anemone-like flowers; tall
'Edulis Superba'	double pink, fragrant; free flowering, good cut flower
'Flame' (*P. lactiflora* x *P. peregrina*)	single, pinky-red; likes partial shade, free flowering, good cut flower
'Kansas'	double, watermelon-red
'Krinkled White'	single, large flowers, delicately textured like tissue paper, pale golden boss of stamens; good cut flower
'Late Windflower'	single, white, anemone-like flower
'Laura Dessert'	double, cream-flushed apricot-yellow; very fragrant
'Little Rhyme'	single, bright red flowers; dissected foliage, low growing, suitable for rockery (very early)
'Lord Kitchener' (syn. 'Balliol')	single, maroon-red
'Miss America'	semi-double, white, fragrant; free flowering
P. officinalis 'Rubra Plena'	double, rich crimson; free flowering
P. tenuifolia 'Rubra Plena'	double, red
'Paula Fay'	semi-double, glowing pink, waxy-textured petals
'Picotee'	single white-edged pinky-mauve petals; lower growing
'Red Charm'	double, rich crimson, dome-shaped flowers; long flowering, tall (early–mid)
'Squeak'	single, cup-shaped, rose-colored blooms; low growing, suitable for rockery (very early)
'Whitleyi Major'	single, ivory-white petals, golden stamens; fragrant; tall

Mid to late-flowering varieties

'Albert Crousse'	double, pink, fragrant
'Alice Harding'	double, creamy-white large blooms, fragrant; tall (late)

BELOW: 'Hermione', late.
BOTTOM: 'Quality Folk', early.

'Auguste Dessert'	semi-double, clear pink petals paling to silvery white edges, very fragrant, free flowering
'Baroness Schroeder'	double, white, globe-shaped blooms, fragrant; good cut flower, free flowering, tall
'Cornelia Shaylor'	double, flushed rose-pink turning to blush-white; strong stems, fragrant
'Duchesse de Nemours'	double, white, fragrant, strong stems; introduced in France in 1856, popular cut flower in Holland
'Edith Cavell'	double, white, fragrant
'Emperor of India'	single, dark purple-pink, self-colored, yellow-tipped stanodes; free flowering
'Félix Crousse'	double, dark red, fragrant; good cut flower
'Festiva Maxima'	double, white with crimson flecks, fragrant; a favorite since its introduction in 1851
'Gardenia'	loosely double, white flowers, gold stamens; fragrant (late)
'Globe of Light'	bright rose-pink, fragrant; tall, free flowering, good cut flower, long flowering season, anemone form
'Karl Rosenfeld'	large, very double cerise-red bloom
'Kelway's Glorious'	double, white-streaked red, very fragrant
'Kelway's Supreme'	semi-double, pink, very fragrant
'Lord Kitchener'	single, red; tall upright variety
'Madame Calot'	double, pink, very fragrant
'Monsieur Jules Elie'	double, luscious pink with up-curving petals, fragrant
'Mrs. Franklin D. Roosevelt'	double, pink, fragrant; good cut flower, free flowering (late)
'Sarah Bernhardt'	double, ruffled, rose-pink blooms; free flowering, tall (very late)
'Sea Shell'	single, mauve-pink, fragrant; good cut flower (late)
'Shirley Temple'	double, ruffled, pink buds fading to cream and blush, strong stems; long flowering, free flowering, good cut flower
'Top Brass'	double, creamy-pink, with a very full center (late)
'Topeka Garnet'	single, dark red, daisy-like flower

Long-flowering varieties
'Baroness Schroeder'
'The Bride'
'Cytherea'
'Duchesse de Nemours'
'Globe of Light'
'James Kelway'
'Jeanne D'Arc'
'Kelway's Lovely'
'Kelway's Supreme'
'Madame Calot'
'Monsieur Jules Elie'
'Philippe Rivoire'
'Queen Alexandra'
'Red Charm'
'Reine Hortense'
'Sarah Bernhardt'
'Shirley Temple'
'Thérèse'

'Salmon Beauty', early.

'Hesperus', mid-season.

Good cut-flower herbaceous varieties

Early

'Bridal Gown'	bomb form, clear white
'Coral Charm'	double, deep pink-coral fading to peachy-cream
'Coral Sunset'	semi-double, coral-pink fading to creamy-lemon
'Charlie's White'	bomb form, white
'Miss America'	double, blush white
'Pink Hawaiian Coral'	double, coral fading to soft pink
'Red Charm'	bomb form, deep crimson

Mid

'Avalanche'	double, creamy-white, hint of pink
'Bowl of Cream'	double, creamy-white
'Bridal Icing'	bomb form, creamy-white
'Chippewa'	double, dark red
'Dr. Alexander Fleming'	double, bright pink
'Gardenia'	double, ruffled, white
'Honey Gold'	double, creamy-white
'Maestro'	very double, brilliant red
'Mrs. F. D. Roosevelt'	double, shell pink
'Pillow Talk'	double, pink
'Princess Margaret'	double, rosy-pink
'Shirley Temple'	double, ruffled, pink fading to cream
'Top Brass'	double, creamy pinky-white

Late

'Ann Cousins'	closely packed double, white
'Best Man'	double, deep red
'Cheddar Cheese'	very double, ruffled, creamy-white
'Cheddar Surprise'	semi-double, white with golden petalodes
'Chiffon Parfait'	double, pink
'Félix Crousse'	double, crimson
'Hermione'	double apple-blossom pink
'Kelway's Glorious'	double, creamy-white with crimson streaks
'Lady Alexander Duff'	double, blush-pink
'Minuet'	double, light pink
'Moon River'	double, creamy-pink
'My Pal Rudy'	very double, warm pink
'Nick Shaylor'	very double, creamy-pink
'Sarah Bernhardt'	double, deep pink, paling on maturity

Selected tree peony cultivars

'Age of Gold'	creamy, lemon, semi-double flowers showing red flares at the base of the ruffled petals
'Alice Harding'	double lemon flowers; nongrafted, old tree peony; can be propagated by division
'Alice Palmer'	open flowers, mauve petals edged with white; vigorous plant
'Cardinal Vaughan'	large semi-double blooms that resemble a rose, ruby-purple petals with silvery margin
'Chromatella'	double, yellow, full-petaled hanging flowers, rose-edged petals
'Chun Ge'	large single flower, petals pale pink with burgundy tip (mid–late)
'Duchess of Kent'	semi-double, open flowers of clear bright rose, paler shade at petal edge; free flowering when young
'Duchess of Marlborough'	huge, silvery-pink, slightly frilly flowers, fully petaled but with an open center
'Duchesse de Morny'	large semi-double flowers, petals pale rose with lavender hints; one of the oldest and most widespread French varieties (early)
'Fen(g) Dan Bai' ('Phoenix White')	white, semi-double flowers with dense fragrance; a cultivar close to the species *P. ostii*
'Fen(g) Dan Fen' ('Phoenix Pink')	pale pink, semi-double flowers with dense fragrance; a cultivar close to the species *P. ostii*

Some fragrant herbaceous peonies

P. emodi
'Albert Crousse'
'Alice Harding'
'Auguste Dessert'
'Baroness Schroeder'
'Bowl of Beauty'
'Burma Ruby'
'Cornelia Shaylor'
'Duchesse de Nemours'
'Edith Cavell'
'Edulis Superba'
'Félix Crousse'
'Festiva Maxima'
'Gardenia'
'Globe of Light'
'Instituteur Doriat'
'Kelway's Glorious'
'Kelway's Supreme'
'Laura Dessert'
'Madame Calot'
'Miss America'
'Monsieur Jules Elie'
'Pink Hawaiian Coral'
'Sea Shell'
'White Sands'
'Whitleyi Major'

'Fujizome-goromo'	pale pink flowers the color of old silk, darker at the center, fully petaled with an open center of "old gold," silvery-blue dissected foliage
'Glory of Huish'	bright scarlet, semi-double blooms opening to show golden center
'Godaishu' ('Five Large Countries')	semi-double flowers, huge pure white petals, slightly bending (mid-season)
'Golden Bowl'	single blooms, up to 4 in. (10 cm) in diameter, lemon-yellow with red flares; bright green dissected foliage (late)
'Hana Kisoi'	enormous semi-double flower, clear pink-rose petals (early)
'Haruno-akebono'	white, semi-double flowers with a central flare of pinky-red
'Koshino-yuki'	green buds opening to huge, double, glistening white flowers
'Kamada-Fuji'	semi-double, large flowers of lilac-mauve, gold center; long-lasting
'Mikunino-akebno'	large single blooms of pure white, irregularly fringed at the edges, to create unusual "ragged" (but appealing) appearance; attractive foliage
'Mrs. Shirley Fry'	single to semi-double blooms of pure white with golden centers; elegantly simple
'Mrs. William Kelway'	semi-double, satiny-white blooms; a ravishingly beautiful plant in flower
'Nigata Akashigata'	double, evocatively beautiful, pale pink flowers with deep magenta stripe through the center of each petal; robust blooms open small and develop in size and color over several days; spectacular blooms
'Reine Elizabeth'	double, huge, fully petaled blooms of deep salmon-pink; traditional Chinese-French hybrid style with heavy hanging flowers
'Renkaku'	pure white, dinner plate–sized, semi-double blooms with golden centers; always popular
'Renown'	single, camellia-like flowers of coppery-orange; deeply dissected leaves with a darker margin as they first unfold
'Rinpo'	luscious, large, semi-double blooms that open very flat; unusual lilac-purple color with silvery-edged petal

'Shima Daijin'	large, purple-red, semi-double flowers (early)
'Shimane Chojuraku'	huge double flowers of lilac-pink with deep purple blotch and bright golden centers
'Shimane Hakugan'	elegant semi-double blooms of pure milk-white; central ring of golden stamens surrounds a single red carpel; stunningly simple
'Shintogen'	sweetly scented, single blooms of red-mauve; attracttive dissected foliage; can be enticed into flowering in late winter if grown in gentle heat, early spring in the garden
'Yoyo No Homare' ('King of Peonies')	large double flowers, bright carmine-red petals (early)

Hybrids of *Paeonia lutea*

The crosses between peonies belonging to the moutan group and *Paeonia delavayi* and its subspecies *P. lutea* and *P. potaninii* are usually called "*Lutea* hybrids." These hybrids have some characteristics that make them quite different from the Japanese, Chinese and French varieties belonging to the moutan (suffruticosa) group: i.e., the yellow or variegated flowers of many varieties, their rapid growth, their remarkable vigor and their late flowering.

'Alhambra' (Saunders 1948)	enormous semi-double flower, petals yellow with some purple at the base; bright green leaves (late)
'Black Pirate' (Saunders 1941)	single flower, petals bright and large, very dark red with black flared base (mid-season)
'Chinese Dragon' (Saunders 1950)	single flower with large crimson petals; rounded edges curl back exposing yellow stamens (early)
'Gauguin' (Daphnis 1965)	long-lasting and unusual single flowers of light raspberry-red, flushed on the back and inside base of the petals with pale gold, red center, very floriferous (early)
'Golden Bowl' (Saunders 1949)	large single flower, golden petals with red flares at base (mid–late)
'Golden Hind' (Saunders 1948–50)	double flower, creamy-yellow petals with purple center (late)
'Gold Sovereign' (Saunders 1950)	semi-double golden flower, petals and stamens creamy-yellow (late)
'Harvest' (Saunders 1948–50)	semi-double flower, petals wheat-yellow with a hint of pink and a red base (late)

Some tree peonies recommended for zone 9
'Coral Terrace', 'Grand Duke Dressed in Blue and Purple', 'Green Dragon Lying on a Chinese Ink Stone', 'Luoyang Red', 'Necklace with Precious Pearls', 'Number One Scholar's Red', 'Phoenix White', 'Rouge Red', 'Taoist Stove Filled with the Pills of Immortality', 'Twin Beauty', 'Zhao Pink'.

Some tree peonies recommended for zone 4
'Black Dragon Holds a Splendid Flower', 'Champion Pink', 'Colorful Painting', 'Coral Terrace', 'Luoyang Red', 'Night Glow on the Sacred Mountain', 'Sunrise Red', 'Supreme Pink'.

'Black Panther', an American hybrid tree peony, opens to luscious black flower.

Big, bold and bragging.

'Hesperus' (Saunders 1948–50)	single flower, pale rose petals with creamy-yellow flares (mid)
'High Noon' (Saunders 1952)	single, cup-shaped flower, lemon-yellow with orange-red base; very early, sometimes repeats in late summer
'Marchioness' (Saunders 1942)	single flowers, apricot petals with pink flares and dark red stamens (late)
'Roman Gold' (Saunders 1941)	single flowers, gold-yellow petals, bright red flares at base (mid)
'Savage Splendor' (Saunders 1950)	single flowers, pale yellow petals with marked veins varying from pink to purple (mid)
'Souvenir du Professeur Maxime Cornu' (Henry 1907)	huge double flowers, ruffled and separated petals, yellow with salmon-pink veins and edges; one of the oldest and most famous hybrids of *Paeonia lutea* (mid)
'Thunderbolt' (Saunders 1948)	single long-lasting flowers, silky black-crimson petals and yellow stamens (early)
'Vesuvian' (Saunders 1948)	dripping with large, deep maroon semi-double flowers; finely cut foliage on compact bush (mid–late)

Appendix 2: Organizations and Suppliers

Organizations

The American Peony Society
Contact: Claudia Schroer
713 White Oak Lane
Gladstone, MO 64116-4607, USA
www.americanpeonysociety.org
info@americanpeonysociety.org

The Canadian Peony Society
PO Box 69507
109 Thomas Street
Oakville, ON L6J 7R4, Canada
www.peony.ca
admin@peony.ca

The Peony Society
(Formerly the British Peony Society)
www.paeonia.org
www.peonysociety.org

Suppliers
United States

A1 Nursery
2842 Fremont Avenue
Shenandoah, IA 51601
Phone: (712) 534-2595
Fax: (801) 740-3838
E-mail: rogerj@coin.heartland.net

A & D Peony & Perennial Nursery
6808 180th S.E.
Snohomish, WA 98290
Phone: (206) 668-9690

Adelman Peony Gardens
5690 Brooklake Road N.E.
PO Box 9193 Salem, OR 97305

Phone: (503) 393-6185
www.peonyparadise.com
E-mail: info@peonyparadise.com

Brothers Herbs & Tree Peonies Inc.
PO Box 1370
Sherwood, OR 97140
Phone: (503) 625-7548
Fax: (503) 625-1667
www.treony.com
E-mail: rick@treony.com

Busse Gardens
17160 245th Avenue
Big Lake, MN 55309
Phone: (800) 544-3192
Fax: (763) 263-1013
www.bussegardens.com

Caprice Nursery
10944 Mill Creek Road S.E.
Aumsville, OR 97325
Phone: (503) 749-1397
Fax: 749-4097
www.capricenursery.com

Countryman Peony Farm
818 Winch Hill Road
Northfield, VT 05663
Phone: (802) 485-8421
Fax: (802) 485-8422

Cricket Hill Garden
670 Walnut Hill Garden
Thomaston, CT 06787
Phone: (860) 283-1042
Toll free: 1-877-723-6642

Fax: (860) 283-5508
www.treepeony.com
E-mail: crickethill@treepeony.com

Gilbert H. Wild & Son
PO Box 338
Sarcoxie, MO 64862-0338
Phone: (888) 449-4537
www.gilberthwild.com

Golden Port International
22129 N.E. 140th Way
Woodinville, WA 98077
Phone: (425) 869-1870
Toll free: 1-877-PEONIES
Fax: (425) 861-5710
www.goldenport.com
E-mail: peony@goldenport.com

Hollingsworth Peonies
28747 290th Street
Maryville, MO 64468
Phone: (660) 562-3010
Fax: (660) 582-8688
www.hollingsworthpeonies.com
E-mail: hpeonies@asde.net

Nature's Promise
PO Box 1164
Tumtum, WA 99034
Phone: (509) 276-8319
www.naturespromise.com
E-mail: cascade@televar.com

The New Peony Farm
PO Box 18235
St. Paul, MN 55118
Phone: (651) 457-8994
www.newpeonyfarm.com

Reath's Nursery
N-195 County Road 577
Vulcan, MI 49892
Phone: (906) 563-9777

'Orange Cup', an attractive garden subject.

www.reathsnursery.com
E-mail: reathnur@up.net

Rice Creek Gardens Inc.
11506 Highway 65
Blaine, MN 55434
Phone: (763) 754-8090
www.ricecreekgardens.com

Sevald Nursery
4937 3rd Avenue South
Minneapolis, MI 55409

Sherman Nursery Company
PO Box 579
Charles City, IA 50616-0579
Toll-free phone: 1-800-747-5980
Fax: (641) 228-7569
E-mail: sales@shermannursery.com

Smirnow's Son's Peonies
168 Maple Hill Road
Huntington, NY 11743
Phone: (631) 421-0836
Fax: (631) 421-0818
E-mail: smirnowb@ix.netcom.com

Song Sparrow Perennial Farm (Roy Klehm)
13101 East Rye Road
Avalon, WI 53505
Toll-free phone: 1-800-553-3715
Fax: (608) 883-2257
www.songsparrow.com
E-mail: info@songsparrow.com

Tomorrow's Treasures
PO Box 434
Black Eagle, MT 59414

Canada
La Pivoinerie D'Aoust
Box 220
Hudson Heights, QC J0P 1J0
Phone: (450) 458-2759
Fax: (450) 458-0253
www.paeonia.com
E-mail: lindsay.daoust@paeonia.com

Pacific Rim Native Plant Nursery
PO Box 413
Chilliwack, BC V2P 6J7
Phone: (604) 792-9279
Fax: (604) 792-1891
www.hillkeep.ca
E-mail: plants@hillkeep.ca

Whitehouse Perennials
594 Rae Rd., R.R.2
Almonte, ON K0A 1A0
Phone: (613) 256-3406
Fax: (613) 256-6827
www.whitehouseperennials.com
E-mail: suzanne@whitehouseperennials.com

United Kingdom
Claire Austin Hardy Plants Ltd.
The Stone House, Coppice Green Lane
Cramp Pool, Shifnal
Shropshire, TF11 8PE
Phone: +44 (1952) 463-700
Fax: +44 (1952) 463-111

www.claireaustin-hardyplants.co.uk
E-mail: enquiries@claireaustin-hardyplants.co.uk

Kelways Ltd.
Barrymore Farm, Langport
Somerset, TA10 9EZ
Phone: +44 (1458) 250-521
Fax: +44 (1458) 253-351
www.kelways.co.uk
E-mail: sales@kelways.co.uk

Phedar Nursery
42 Bunkers Hill, Romiley
Stockport, SK6 3DS
Phone/Fax: +44 (161) 430-3772
www.phedar.com

Germany
Albrecht Hoch
Postfach 370460
Ahornstraße 2a,
D-1000 Berlin 37 (Zehlendorf)

Heinz Klose
Rosenstrasse 10
D-34253 Lohfelden, Frankfurt
Phone: +49 561-515555
Fax: +49 561-515120
www.staudengaertner-klose.de

Päonien Garten
Am Steinberg 11
60437 Frankfurt am Main
Phone/Fax: +49 6101-541466
www.paeoniengarten.de
E-mail: pg@parlasca.de

Staudengärtnerei Gräfin von Zeppelin
Weinstrasse 2
D-79295 Sulzburg-Laufen/Baden
Phone: +49 7634-69716
Fax: +49 7634-6599
www.graefin-v-zeppelin.com
E-mail: info@graefin-v-zeppelin.com

New Zealand

Marsal Peonies
Old South Road
R.D. Dunsandel, Canterbury
Phone/Fax: +64 3 325-4003

Tony and Judy Banks
Omeo Peonies
6 Hawley Road
R.D.1, Alexandra
Phone: +64 3 449-2097

Simmons Peonies
389 Buchanans Road
R.D. 6, Christchuch 8004
Phone: +64 3 342-1160
Fax: +64 3 342-1162
www.peony.net.nz
E-mail: p.e.simmons@clear.net.nz

Southern Charm Paeonies
Seaforth Road
R.D. 3, Timaru
Phone/Fax: +64 3 615-9389
www.southerncharm.co.nz
E-mail: info@southerncharm.co.nz

The Peony Gardens
671 Ellis Road
3 R.D., Lumsden
Phone: +64 25 220-7879
www.thepeonygardens.co.nz
E-mail: info@thepeonygardens.co.nz

Dot and John McFarlane
Tree Paeonies
9 R.D., Waimate
Phone: +64 3 689-4865
Fax: +64 3 689-4867
www.paeonies.net.nz

France

Pivoines Rivière
"La Plaine", 26400 Crest, France
Phone: +33 4 75.25.44.85
Fax: +33 4 75.76.77.38
www.pivoinesriviere.com

Australia

Peony Garden
283 Little Lonsdale Street
Melbourne, Victoria 3000
www.peonygarden.com.au
E-mail: peonygarden@hotmail.com

Bibliography

Campbell-Culver, Maggie. *The Origin of Plants.* London: Headline Book Publishing, 2001.

Chevalier, Andrew. *The Encyclopedia of Medicinal Plants.* London: Dorling Kindersley, 1996.

Fearnley-Whittingstall, Jane. *Peonies: The Imperial Flower.* London: Weidenfeld & Nicolson, 1999.

Genders, Roy. *The Peony.* London: John Gifford, 1961.

Grieve, Mrs. M. *A Modern Herbal.* London: Tiger Books International, 1994.

Hadfield, Miles. *Pioneers in Gardening.* London: Bloomsbury, 1996.

Harding, Alice. *The Peony.* London: B.T. Batsford, 1993.

Haworth-Booth, Michael. *The Moutan or Tree Peony.* London: Constable Publishers, 1963.

Nehrling, Arno, and Irene Nehrling. *Peonies: Outdoors and In.* New York: Dover Publications, 1975.

Robinson, William. *The English Flower Garden.* London: Bloomsbury, 1883 (1996 edition).

Rogers, Allan. *Peonies.* Portland, OR: Timber Press, 1995.

Roper, Lanning. *Hardy Herbaceous Plants.* Harmondsworth, Middlesex: Penguin Books, 1960.

Wister, John C. (editor). *The Peonies.* Washington, DC: The American Horticultural Society, 1962.

Index